GENESIS 1, 2, 3, and Beyond

Journeys Through the Early Universe

GENESIS 1, 2, 3, and Beyond

Journeys Through the Early Universe

**RELIANT
PUBLISHING**
A DIVISION OF REDEMPTION PRESS

Wendell Ford

Published by Reliant Publishing, an imprint of Redemption Press, PO Box 427, Enumclaw, WA 98022.

Toll-Free (844) 2REDEEM (273-3336)

Redemption Press is honored to present this title in partnership with the author. The views expressed or implied in this work are those of the author. Redemption Press provides our imprint seal representing design excellence, creative content, and high-quality production.

ISBN: 978-1-64645-015-2 (Paperback)
       978-1-64645-016-9 (ePub)
       978-1-64645-017-6 (Mobi)

Library of Congress Catalog Card Number: 2019916774

Contents

Preface

MANY BOOKS, ARTICLES, AND PAPERS have been written (and will be written) about the book of Genesis. So why write one more? The answer is simply as an aid to organize and preserve some of my various thoughts that I recently used to teach an adult Bible class and to document a lot of the study I have done over the last 60 years. Most of what I have to say has been said, probably many times over, but over the years, I did not keep track of all the sources I consulted; and many, if not most, of the ideas presented will have been proposed earlier by someone else; therefore, I am unable to give all the credit everywhere it is due. A few of the sources have been read recently enough to still be identified but not always specific ideas. All learning, especially science, is built on the foundation of those who came before. Unless otherwise indicated, all of the scientific theories are taught the in curricula of the science department of schools, are presented in text and other books, can be explored in many web sites. I prefer web sites maintained by universities because they tend to more up-to-date. I have included recently published references on most of the topics I will cover that were written for the general public and thus are very readable. If your interest is piqued, refer to them; after all, those authors spent a great deal of study and effort to make their knowledge available. You might want to buy a book or two. I would suggest starting with the books by John Walton, references 14 and 15, because I refer to them several times.

He has the knowledge and resources to present the subject and does a much job of it than I could.

My background is not as a biblical scholar or an antiquity scholar of any type. Thus I am grateful to those authors who are and who have written to inform those of us who are less educated in these matters. Linguistics, particularly ancient linguistics, is keenly important to this Genesis study. That is why I used reference 17 for my study rather than relying on information found elsewhere. My background is scientific as an electrical engineer working with scientists, especially physicists. Word studies were done using reference 17; it is based on the KJV which is more literal that many recent versions. The process was to check the English word for a passage of interest in the RSV and NIV. If there was reasonable agreement, I then searched the concordance (Ref. 17). Many times there is more than one Hebrew word translated to an English word; reference 17 separates these. If there were fewer than 50 entries, I read them all; otherwise I did a careful sample. Reference 17 also contains a section showing all the ways a given Hebrew word is translated into English. I read most of these as well; occasionally there were interesting surprises (which I won't detail here).

I decided to do a Google search on the book of Genesis. I received a response that said there were over 61 million matches. I did not read all of them or look at very many. Next I did a search of the Library of Congress (LOC). This narrowed the field considerably, as I only received around 8,000 responses; these would probably be only those that contained Genesis in the title. Of these 8,000, over 3,000 have been digitized. I did not read all of these either. All of the numbers are changing daily. The point is that probably all the things I have to say will have already been said by someone else. The references listed are only noteworthy because they are the ones I have most recently consulted. All who have broached the subject of Genesis have as a purpose to make the ideas available to as many others as possible. Some of those messages will be complimentary to Genesis, while others will be derogatory.

I believe there is no other passage in the Bible that has been so misused and abused by believers and nonbelievers alike as the early chapters of Genesis have been. I think this phenomenon comes about because of the tendency to try to make Genesis say much more than God intended. For example, consider the first 25 verses, comprised of between 500 and 600 words. Exactly how much detail can one expect to find in such a brief passage? The science of Information Theory quantifies the amount of information contained in a message based on redundancy, repetition, predictability, and other factors. The technical unit of measurement is a bit. Appling the analysis to Genesis chapter 1 results in very small number of bits of information. This tells us the message was not in conveying details, but something else, which we will examine throughout this book. That message had to be written in a way that it could be understood down through time and through all generations. The intricate details were not important but have been left for humans to discover and understand with the intellect God gave them. When details are important, they are given. For example, compare the details for making the tabernacle or the outlining the laws found in Leviticus and Deuteronomy.

Some say that there is a discrepancy between the Bible, Genesis in particular, and science (which is a pretty broad term). When one considers that the area of interest to both is different, the problems are minimized or eliminated. For example, beginnings are treated in each but from entirely different perspectives. Science is concerned about the details in the "how" of things and often about the exact "when," whereas religion in general and the Bible in particular is concerned about the "who" and the purpose. Science can then determine how things work, how they affect us, make predictions about unknown processes, and generally delve into things not understood. This is very much centered on human's understanding of the material things around them. The biblical view, to sum up, is concerned with people and how they behave and interact. Engineering takes the principles learned in science and uses them to make things useful to people.

Because of my interest in science, I will insert current scientific ideas and theories at various places. The purpose is not to pit science against the Bible but to show the different focus each employs. By looking at both, we can gain a fuller, richer, more comprehensive, and more satisfying appreciation of the world in which we live. In each case the wonder and awe (and respect) of it all is stimulated, but if we lack these things, we lose the perspective of our place in the scheme of things, and our lives lose their meaning.

Too often scientists (or those who listen to them) ridicule or dismiss theology and religion because they see a conflict between religion and science. The scientists refer to religion and its followers as clinging onto obsolete scientific principles or relying on "God of the gaps" arguments. I believe they should not be so smug or arrogant about their accusations or dismissals because a history of science will reveal theories that have been proven wrong, yet have been defended for a long time before acceptance.

Aristotle's science prevailed for centuries. When James Clerk Maxwell developed his field equations for electricity and magnetism, and electromagnetic waves, he proposed something called the aether (there are different spellings of this) that filled all space, including a vacuum. A famous experiment in 1887 disproved its existence. Continental drift and tectonic plates were ridiculed when first proposed but are now accepted. To sum up the progress of science (and other fields) is a quote attributed to Arthur Schopenhauer: "All truth passes through stages. First, it is ridiculed. Second, it is violently opposed. Third, it is accepted as being self-evident." (Cited in reference 9, page 51). Be aware that the treatment of the scientific topics is extremely brief. For more information and detail, refer to the references or the similar works on a particular subject. I will not answer all the questions that you may have about Genesis 1–3, and I will certainly not answer all of mine.

1

How Do We Begin

THIS WILL MAINLY BE A study of the first three chapters of Genesis. To do so will require going far beyond Genesis to gain the background necessary for an understanding. You need to know up front that my background is in engineering and science, which informs the approach I will take. Among other things, this means that I will go off on several tangents at times (even here at the start), but they will be relevant, and then we will get back. I will try to watch for the boredom factor.

I will open with a disclaimer. My purpose is not to necessarily change your mind about any of the things you believe, but rather it is to present a way of approaching your reading of these chapters. Nothing that is presented should detract from the fact that this is the word of God and that there are important things to be learned. It is not like a debate where a point is to be proved or disproved with a winner or loser. It is to develop a way of thinking. Do not let the debate over the trivial details cause you to miss the far deeper message contained in these early chapters. There are profound issues examined that arise, due to the condition of humanity.

The outstanding abuse and misuse of Genesis is to prove or disprove the existence of God. Those coming into the argument already have their minds made up and are seeking verification of their views. (This holds true for so many of the issues concerning the Bible.) I also think that it is a mistake for someone wanting to read the Old Testament for the first time to start reading at Genesis 1:1. The people to whom Genesis was written had a different background than we do, which we need to understand; therefore, I would recommend starting at Genesis 12 and read through at least Exodus and Numbers. Then one can consider the problems that were being addressed. First and foremost, this nomadic people who had just come out of slavery needed to be forged into a nation in order to fulfill the great charge that God had given to Abraham which is ultimately to be fulfilled through them and their descendants (Genesis chapter 15).

I will delve into many areas of science that I feel will help you understand how the science and the Bible can fit together. A contrast will become apparent in style and content because the areas of science and religion simply are not exploring the world from the same perspective, do not have the same tools, and do not have the same purpose. Besides that, I like science (and the Bible). In my lifetime I have seen tremendous changes in science and scientific theories, which I expect to continue. Many times in history, scientists (and others) have thought that all had been explained and their job was done, only to have it completely overthrown. The theory of everything does not exist, and "everything" doesn't include everything.

Contrary to what some may think, I believe the background is important in a study of the Bible. This is because, even though it was written and passed down for our benefit, it was written to a particular people, with a particular language, with a particular culture that are not the same as ours. This is crucial, as it would be impossible to write something that fits in all cultures in all languages for all time. Culture is the way we view life and how we live in it and is far ranging from the food we eat, the work we do, our attitudes, the clothes we wear, down to the way we comb our hair. Too many missionaries have lost effectiveness in witnessing because they tried to convert the people to modern American culture before converting them to the gospel. This is why I want to go off on a lot of tangents. Every book of the Bible was written to specific people and had to have meaning to those people whom we cannot ignore. The language and the culture contribute to the meaning, including prophecies, which may include future events, but could be understood a lot better by the original readers than by us.

We think we understand some old analogies and comparisons better than we really do. One common example is that of a shepherd. We really don't know all the intricacies of being a shepherd in our times let alone in biblical times. In America we don't understand royalty, kingship, or subjection and loyalty to them the same way someone who actually lives under a king (or queen).

As stated in the Preface, I believe that there is no other passage in the Bible more misunderstood, misused, and abused by both believers and nonbelievers alike than the early chapters of Genesis. The reason for this is relating Genesis to our culture, knowledge, and biases instead of looking at it in context; therefore, to do a proper study, forget all you have learned, forget your knowledge of the universe, ignore your culture, and imagine yourself as an Israelite standing at the base of Mount Sinai having just come out of 400 years of captivity. This might seem impossible to do, of course, but try it.

Genesis deals with the Israelites in their culture and their understanding (thus the sun and moon rose and set rather than the earth circling the sun and the moon the earth). We need to ignore our knowledge and try to look at things from the standpoint of the common knowledge of the people at the time of the writing (this would mean 3,000 to 3,500 years ago). They thought the earth was flat if they thought about it at all. They had a simple view of the makeup of the universe. Each culture had its own description of it. One simple model prevalent among the Semitic peoples (Assyrians, Babylonians, Canaanites, Phoenicians, and Hebrews) consisted of three or five layers. The bottom layer was the underworld, the underground, or Sheol. The middle layer was the earth where people lived. The top layer was the heavens, the dwelling place of the gods. Sometimes the five layers included a layer of lower water under the earth (from which wells and springs came) and a layer of upper water above the earth (clouds or rain). The souls of the dead were thought to descend to Sheol; this may have given rise to the custom of burying the body in the earth (the underworld).

A more complicated concept of the seven heavens (of which several variations exist) was also later used. One concept was number one that was below the surface of the earth, number two was the surface of the earth, number three was the atmosphere where the clouds were, number four was the sky (a solid, transparent layer, hence the firmament), number five was the domain of the moon and sun, number six the realm of the stars, and number seven the dwelling place of the gods. (To which do you think Paul is referring to in 2 Cor. 12:1–5)? Any physical descriptions given in Genesis would have been in these terms so that the original readers could grasp the concepts. Today, God has endowed humans with an intellect that they are expected to use to delve into the "how" of things, yet the Bible is dealing with the "who."

Genesis Background

As with the study of any book of the Bible, understanding it is much easier if the background is known and considered. This includes as much information as possible about things such as the author and his background, intended audience, historical setting, original language, purpose for the writing, how it has been regarded since the writing, and contemporary literature. It is not always possible to find all of this information. I remember once having an elder teach a class on one of the minor prophets, perhaps Hosea. The elder proudly announced that we were going to study the book; not study about the book. I found myself very much lost until I finally studied about the book on my own.

I think it is important to study a lot about the book of Genesis to better understand it. A lot of what we know about the book is found in the book, but we will at times have to go far beyond the book to understand it. We may even have to mention the existence of literature, contemporary with Genesis. Also, there are those who say we should not refer to the culture of the times (God is always the same and His word never changes; however, our language changes), but to do so means we are interpreting it in terms of our own culture. You cannot eliminate culture from any literature! The rule to keep in mind is that Genesis was written for us but not to us. (See reference 15, page 9, for an expanded discussion).

Moses is generally accepted as the author of the first five books of the Bible (the Pentateuch). References, including Jesus, both in the Old and New Testaments identify Moses as the giver of the law in what would be these five books (Ezra 3:2; Mal. 4:4; Mark 12:20; 1 Cor. 9:9; and numerous others). We know that he was born in Egypt, raised as Pharaoh's son (with his own mother as his nanny) for 40 years, and educated in the knowledge of Egypt (Acts 7:22), which means he probably spoke and wrote Egyptian and Hebrew. Then he spent 40 years as a wandering shepherd. I suspect that God used this time to wean him off the Egyptian culture. The oldest copies of the Pentateuch that we have today are in Hebrew and are on the order of a thousand years old. The discovery of the Dead Sea scrolls has moved this date back for some OT writings. What we now have are English translations. The English language is always changing, and new versions try to keep up with it.

To more fully understand Genesis, I would categorize the five books of Moses in the following way (this not the result of great detailed study or insight, but simply what I would gather from the content of the books): Genesis, Exodus, and Leviticus were most likely written while the Israelites were still camped at the base of Mount Sinai. After all, this is where the law was given to Moses and he was passing it on. Genesis was to explain how they had gotten to where they were, and contains at least two major sections: chapters 1–11 about how they came to be (and basically answer the question Moses asked in Exodus), while the rest of the book is about the forming (creation) of the Israel nation. Remember, the Israelites were always talking about wanting to go back to Egypt. Regarding the other books in the Pentateuch, Exodus contained the instructions about how they were to conduct business now that they were on their own. Leviticus had the detailed laws. Numbers was written to chronicle their wanderings in the wilderness, and Deuteronomy was written as a farewell and a reminder as they were to enter the promised land without Moses. The preceding points should be kept in mind when reading Genesis 1.

For several centuries there have been varying thoughts about what the early part of Genesis is describing. Before the rise of modern science (which, interestingly enough, was only possible after the acceptance of biblical theology. In most pagan religions, events were controlled by the gods. Each god had its own domain and controlled it. People had to appease the gods in various ways to get what they wanted, or simply please the god to prevent disaster. Biblical theology teaches that God is not capricious, that things are ordered, and that the natural laws of the world are consistent.), religious leaders took the creation story as literal, according to the perspective of the world they observed. They tried to force the science of the day to conform to their views. When discoveries started to result in a different view, conflicts arose.

Most people have some notion of these conflicts and it is not my intent to delve into them. Instead, I want to present some of my thoughts. These were inspired (not in the biblical sense) by reading many works over the last few years. I have been influenced by authors like N. T. Wright, John H. Walton, Alistair McGrath, John D. Barrow, Francis S. Collins, Richard Muller, and many others. I am not sure at this time which ideas I got from whom. If you think something seems to be taken from some author, you are probably right. I have not kept notes to help me identify the source of each idea.

There is ancient literature written about the time of the writing of Genesis. Some of that literature includes events similar to biblical events, especially the Babylonians, who had a well-known creation account. Many writers have suggested that Genesis was really taken from these stories. It does not take much comparison to dispel that idea. The Babylonian story (and all other accounts from this period) is about a multiplicity of gods behaving in very human ways. The contrast is readily apparent. There is also the survival of the Genesis account and the obscurity of other accounts. However, they are useful as an insight into the thinking of peoples in that era. John Walton does an excellent job of discussing these issues (references 14 and 15, numerous places).

The people in the Bible who lived up until the time of Abraham seemed to be isolated individuals and a whole nation was not necessarily involved. (Remember that God told Abraham that he would make of him a great nation.) It is not known what language these early people spoke, nor if they even had a written language. (Even at the time of Moses, lots of Egyptian writings were in the hieroglyphs found in the pyramids and other ruins.) Sometime between Abraham and Moses, the Israelites developed their Hebrew language and writing. Unlike most of the other cultures around them, it appears that most of them (at least the males) were literate. This is evident in the New Testament where even poor fishermen such as Peter and Andrew were literate. Writing is not mentioned in Genesis.

They knew nothing of 21st century cosmology or science. The purpose of the Bible was not to bring them up to 21st century understanding of those topics.

A key (and very revealing) verse for the study of Genesis is found in Exodus 3:13 when Moses said to God, "If I come to the people of Israel and say to them, 'The God of your fathers has sent me to you,' and they ask me, 'What is his name?' what shall I say to them?" (RSV). Why did Moses have to ask this question? God has been with them from Abraham to Joseph and their going into Egypt. For 400 years, they have been exposed to the Egyptian culture and gods. All cultures except those derived from the Judeo-Christian background were/are polytheistic. It even took the Israelites a long time to accept the existence of only one god. Hence, they tended to drift off into idolatry. Polytheism still existed in NT times as Paul learned in his visit to Athens (Acts 17:15ff); therefore, people under polytheism did not have the concept we use of there being a "spiritual realm" and a "physical realm." All physical phenomena were simply the gods exercising control over their particular area. Examples of Israel's actually believing that some of the gods really did have power is seen in a couple of interesting cases: in Genesis 31:17–35 when Rachel stole the household gods of Laban and in Joshua chapter 7 when Achan took some gods from Jericho. (See also Judg. 17:1–6.)

In the Bible, an entirely different view is given. Humans are created in the image of God, and, in a way, represent Him on earth. Thus all of creation is tailored for the benefit of humans. God is consistent. What happens is not based on His whims or moods (except special cases for special purposes, such as the flood). Thus humans can count on the world always operating the same way in which God has assigned a function to the physical elements, and humans continue to fulfill it. The creation in Genesis is about the establishment of an environment intended for human occupation.

We will start with Genesis 1:1: "In the beginning, God created the heavens and the earth" (NIV, RSV). There are a lot of assumptions with this verse which aren't really there, as it does not say that the creation was out of nothing. That language is adapted from Hebrews 11:3 and Romans 4:17. (It doesn't say it wasn't either.) There is no indication of the time period involved. The entire physical universe is created in Genesis 1:1. Nothing is told about what things were like before. A fraction of a second or even billions of years could have happened before we get to verse two. The verse does not address all the questions that we raise about the creation process. It has only one point, that it was God who was responsible for creation, not the gods of the Egyptians or other peoples. We are interested in the who, not the what. After all, it is a very short verse and we should expect no detail.

All in all this is a very simple verse that in only ten words covers a lot of ground, so to speak. Skeptics have long attacked this verse with questions such as "Where did God come from?" and "What was there before?" Now, as we shall see, we can ask similar questions of them that are just as unanswerable. To do so, I will trace the development of cosmological ideas up to the present. There can be new theories and new discoveries to come that will alter the theories. This has been happening all along, so why expect it to stop? I read most of the material to be presented from many different sources over time. An excellent source for someone who is interested in more details is found in the in the book by Richard Muller (reference 9) and a very good history of cosmology in the book by Anna Frebel (reference 21). They would be very sound investments, but like all writings on cosmology, it can become quickly out of date.

There is no reason why we cannot look at what current science tells about what was happening or had happened during the time covered by verses one and two. One point we need to keep in mind is that our concept of time and our obsession with observing it did not exist during these two verses. An equally important point is that science is an ever-changing landscape. Therefore, we will trace some of the developments through history. These will include things like cosmology, geology, and physics. It is ironic that today, the largest and the smallest of bodies turn out to be linked. The very matter makeup in the atomic realm contains processes that are important in the forming of stars.

Science in OT times was quite different from what we are used to now, with the most notable difference being that it did not depend on experiments, but was the purview of philosophers and other thinkers. Aristotle believed that all truth could be obtained by reason alone. This system lasted well into the second millennium AD. If anyone thought about it at all, they thought the earth was flat. The cosmologies considered the earth as the center of the universe. Around the earth were layers that held the observed bodies. There were many manifestations of this idea with varying number of layers, called "heavens," and seven seemed to be a popular number. These ideas have been mentioned earlier.

The middle of the first millennium BC gave rise to famous Greek philosophers and mathematicians. Aristotle is the most famous of these, and his science was the standard because the Roman church accepted his views as basic doctrine. In the fourth century AD, Augustine expanded somewhat and propagated the doctrine. During this time, theories were strictly logical exercises with no thought to check them by experimentation, and naturally, there were a few deviations, such as an object in water displaced the same volume of water as itself. Others noticed some curvature to the earth by watching how ships appeared and disappeared on the horizon.

Copernicus and Galileo are the most known to have broken away from the idea of an earth-centered universe, and they received a lot of criticism from the existing scientific community and strong opposition from the Roman church. They led the way from an earth-centered solar system to one with the sun at the center with the planets orbiting around it. Galileo's telescope also provided many startling discoveries such as moons around other planets. The possibility that the stars were like the sun, but much farther away, was disturbing to the status quo. Gradually, astronomy became a legitimate field of inquiry and morphed into cosmology.

Isaac Newton's publication of his mathematical theory of mechanical laws around 1687 provided the framework for explaining planetary motions as well as the terrestrial interactions between bodies. The laws were very successful for describing and predicting the behavior of numerous phenomena. Based on that success, many believed that all behavior could be explained by application of these laws, including biology and human behavior. All that was needed was to know the initial conditions and then the future could be determined. In other words, they thought the theory of everything had been discovered. One area not covered by Newton was that of electricity and magnetism. Natural magnetism was known in the form called lodestone, and static electricity and lightning were believed to be related. Others were experimenting with batteries and other simple electrical devices.

Around 1865 a Scottish physicist, James Maxwell, came up with equations showing that electricity and magnetism were basically the same force. His equations form the basis for electrical engineering, and later, electronics; his equations also showed how a magnetic field can be produced by passing an electric current through a coil and how a moving conductor in a magnetic field produces an electric current. Rapid advances were made in the use of electricity. Motors and generators could be designed that were much more convenient than steam for powering machinery.

All of these discoveries, along with Charles Darwin's theory of evolution, had an impact on how people viewed Genesis. Unfortunately, too many religious leaders had tied their theology to contemporary science rather than sticking to the Scriptures. As science advanced, much of that theology became obsolete, including much of the interpretation of Genesis 1. This book is an effort to show that the connecting of Scripture and scientific theories is not a proper use of either and does not mean that one cannot inform the other. The Bible simply does not deal with intricate details of the physical and how it came to be.

The last 150 years or so have seen tremendous changes in scientific inquiries. Ironically, this is most apparent in the extremes of the very large and the very small, compared to the scale of humans. They both rely on indirect observations and are surprisingly related. The very small is discussed in the Appendix.

Cosmology has gone through several different concepts as to the nature of the universe. The first serious studies proposed the universe was static, never changing; this coincided with the observations that could be made throughout a human lifespan. Better instruments and better techniques showed that the stars were actually moving with respect to each other. Not only that, but in 1929, Edwin Hubble discovered that the universe was actually expanding. The concept took a while for all astronomers to get on board. As late as 1955, in Frontiers of Astronomy, author Fred Hoyle proposed a universe in which expansion was an illusion, wherein matter was continually being created and destroyed. The theory to explain the expansion, first proposed by George Gamow and Ralph Alpher, was not believed by Hoyle, and he ridiculed it, calling it the Big Bang. Gamow liked the name and so it has stuck. Basically the idea is that the universe began at a single point of infinite mass and zero volume called a singularity. (The Catholic Church officially accepted the Big Bang as doctrine in 1952.)

One of the things arising from Einstein's general theory of relativity is that space and time are linked together in a four-dimensional continuum called space-time and that time and space can no longer be considered separately. He also considered space to be flexible like a rubber sheet. The explosion at the Big Bang then was not just an expansion of matter but of space itself. (Then you have to ask the question, "Exactly what is space anyway"?) The matter merely got carried along with it. The same can be said for time. Observations have shown that every galaxy in the universe is moving away from each one. The farther away they are, the faster their movement. The latest shows that the rate of movement is accelerating. An analogy would be taking a non-inflated balloon, covering the skin with dots, and then blowing it up therefore showing how the dots appear to be moving away from each other. If the whole volume is imagined having dots throughout the interior, those on the surface can be seen moving faster than those near the center of the volume. One important difference between a balloon and the universe is that the force inflating a balloon (blowing air into it) is known as well as its point of origin. Not so with the universe. Much current research and many theories study the force, which causes the universe to expand. Analogies are never satisfactory on all points!

The enormity of the universe is unfathomable. Each galaxy is made up of billions of stars with a high density core, and the universe made up of billions of galaxies. The numbers are truly astronomical. The insignificance of the earth becomes apparent. However, the irony of relativity, according to one of my reference books, is that relativity can return to the earth being at the center of the universe, as well as any other point in the universe. From our standpoint, the only reference that matters is where we are and in a practical sense might as well be the center of the universe.

Now, due to the Big Bang, scientists have the same dilemma that they were trying to pin on Genesis. What exactly was the singularity that started the process? What was there before? Where did it come from? What caused it to start? As answers cannot be detected, the same evasions can be evoked: There was no there, there, and no then, then, and no before, before.

2

The Background

IN CHAPTER 1, I STATED the idea that Genesis 1:1 included creation of all the material things in the universe with no time span given. Just a couple more tangents before proceeding to verse 2 and further are in order.

The general rules of biblical interpretation are extremely important when looking at the early chapters of Genesis. The Genesis that we have was written in the Hebrew language 3,500 or so years ago. The oldest copies are about 1,000 years old. For me to read it, I must rely on translations into English. The translation process often encounters words that are obscure with no extra biblical writings to help determine the meaning or nuance. Even English has, and continues to, experienced tremendous changes. Five hundred years ago, the English language was considerably different from today's English. Therefore, one must be careful to not put too much emphasis on the translator(s)'s choice of English words, especially the more obscure or rare Hebrew words. An important point to remember is that an English word that appears in both the OT and NT are translating from different languages. The words from Hebrew and Greek may not have exactly the same meaning, and neither may be fully represented by the chosen English word. Though usually not a big problem, it certainly exists.

Next we must suspend our view and knowledge of the world and beyond. We need to think in terms of how the people at the time of the writing viewed things. This may be an impossible task but the effort must be made.

Next we must determine the type of book the Bible is. It is too often viewed in the wrong way. We know what it is not. It is not a science textbook; it is not a complete history; it is not merely a rule book; and it is not a "cookbook," although in some sense it may be all of these. It is more about the "who" than about the "what" and tells the story of God's relationship with humans through the medium of specific people. Various people are chosen at times for a specific purpose (or mission, if you will). All of the other things are simply the background against which God's purpose is carried out. The description of things is such that people to whom it is written would understand them as they viewed the world. The insistence on the literal interpretation of many of the events and activities is often made stronger by those trying to discredit the Bible, because they believe it strengthens their case, than by those who actually believe it. Unfortunately, too many believers have fallen prey to this tactic and try to defend something that is not really present.

In Genesis 1, the first thing we come across is the concept of creation. The Hebrew word is bara that occurs about 50 times in the OT and is the only word translated as create. Many volumes have been written on this and many more will be. The popular concept has been that to create means nothing was there, and then something is there. Verses like Hebrews 11:3 are cited as proof; however, a careful reading of the verse does not demand this. Perhaps our use in English, such as an artist creating a work, is closer to the idea, and more like Psalms 51:10 that says, "Create in me a new heart" (KJV).

Careful reading of the first chapters of Genesis does not require the "making something from nothing" concept. Chapter 1 is not concerned with the material aspects of creation but rather who is responsible for it. Verse two is significant in describing the earth as without form. This is a difficult verse to translate because the English words don't quite convey the same concept. The Hebrew verb tohu occurs 20 times. Examining the usage is necessary to understand the concept. (John Walton does an extensive analysis of bara and tohu in reference 15, pages 38 to 53). The rest of chapter 1 is concerned with applying form and function as the meaning of creation. Creation is when something becomes fully operational and not just when the material structure is formed. An example today would be setting up a hospital. When is it created? Is it when the construction is approved? Is it when the plans are drawn or when the funding is approved? Is it when the building shell is completed or the interior is finished? Is it when the equipment is installed? When the staff is hired and on board, or when the first patients are admitted and treated? We cannot really describe it as being created until it is fully functioning. (See also the discussion of John Walton in reference 15, pages 23 to 28).

The creation of the earth and the universe can be considered in the same way. Genesis is describing the creation of the earth until it is fully functional, fit for human habitation. Sure, God could have done it in an instant but what would be the point? Why would there be a need to hurry? Why not let the processes that scientists have proposed operate according to the laws God has created? The description of something being "good" means that it is performing as designed and working properly. Something "not good" was man being alone (Gen. 2:18); hence, woman was created. There is no indication of how the material creation was done or how long it took.

To see that this is so, look at the "days." (See the next chapter for a discussion on the concept of time.) The activities described have as the end result that the earth is made suitable for human habitation. The material things are not gods as the prevailing cultures suppose, but are provided for human's use.

There are a lot of ideas about the seven days and what is meant by them. As for me I believe all of them. On the other hand I don't believe any of them. By this I mean that these theories were formulated by the perspective of the person who generated them, and they mean something helpful to that person. They probably don't mean much to anyone else. I want to stick to the deeper message and to the perspective of the people to whom Genesis was written, although it will be hard to do the latter at times. I believe that the hang up about the length of time is irrelevant and meant to be a distraction from the message conveyed; rather, it is because of the changes in the ideas about cosmology and universe in the last 500 years, and the desire to know exactly how everything came to be and works, that there is a problem. There are constant changes in the scientific ideas of astronomy and cosmology going on today.

Genesis chapter 1 needs to be dealt with as a whole before being absorbed by details of each "day." As for the Israelite 3,000 years ago, the actual amount of time is not the issue. Remember that at the time, the belief was that multiple gods had a direct and immediate hand in controlling everything, and that even some things were actual gods, like the sun and the moon. Genesis is written to dispel that by presenting the one and only true God and that He considers Israel as His special nation for a special purpose. (We are the beneficiaries of that purpose, namely Christ.)

The acts of creation were done in an orderly way. The progression is such that each act is built upon the previously created things. Ultimately each creation was preparing the earth as a suitable habitat for humanity. The created things were not gods in themselves. Notice that each of the things in some culture at some time or another was worshipped as a god. But at the end of creation, humans (Gen. 1:28) are to have dominion over everything; that shows that things are not gods, nor are they controlled by them. I believe that this mandate also implies that knowledge about the earth and all it contains is not given immediately to humans but that part of subduing it is learning all about it and putting that knowledge to use.

After the universe is created in Genesis 1:1 and the beginning condition of the earth is described in 1:2; the preparation of the earth is given in the rest of the chapter. Notice the format of the chapter: after the first two verses, it is divided into six passages. Because the first two verses are outside the descriptions of the seven days, limiting creation to seven literal days would omit the first two verses. A lot of time could have passed (and evidently did) in those two verses. This is not the same as saying there was a big gap in between; it was a continuous process flowing into the rest of chapter 1. Each passage begins with God bringing something into existence and ends with "and there was evening, and there was morning—the [first] day" (NIV). To me this signifies that all of the activity took place before the designated day. That is why it says "evening," meaning the end of the work, and then "morning," meaning a new activity can be started. There is no time indicated for how long the activity before the "evening" took to be accomplished. The days need not be consecutive. They can be the time of assigning functions as suggested by John Walton (reference 15) and still understood as a normal day by the people to whom Genesis is written. This could also explain why there is no evening and morning mentioned on the seventh day. God is resting from His work of creation because the work is finished. In this scenario there is no conflict to whatever times or dates the geologists, paleontologists, and others assign to the age of the earth.

Day 1 has light and darkness including an evening and morning even though the sun is not mentioned until Day 4. However, there were plenty of light sources in the universe. Why is the "light" called "day" and not just left as "light"? Light is not something we think of as being "created." It is a form of energy that is always traveling and is not seen until it strikes an object. (We will see later that it can behave as a particle with zero rest mass). Neither is "darkness" created; it is simply the absence of light (and hence, no energy). Without light everything would be dark, and light is the essential energy source for all life.

Day 2 talks about the separation of water on the earth and the water above (possibly clouds?). Water is a necessary substance for life as we know it, which is why it is much sought after on earth and elsewhere in the universe. The term firmament reflects the ancient's idea that the sky was solid. Day 3 describes the emergence of dry land from water and the rise of vegetation. This would imply that originally, much of the surface of the earth was covered with water. This does not have to be true if it is only functions that are being assigned. Vegetation requires the sun for photosynthesis whose function is not assigned until the next day. On Day 4, the sun and the moon are given their functions. What is really being created is a way for humans to track time. Sea creatures and birds appear on Day 5. Finally, all other living things appear on Day 6. There is no description of how the things on Day 6 came about; only that they came forth from the earth.

Before examining the passages in detail, I want to look at the current scientific understanding of a couple of concepts that we take for granted and assume we understand when we really do not. The information will be greatly condensed from my life-long study of science much of which is given in the references; refer to them and other sources for a more comprehensive treatment. Particle physics and cosmology are rapidly changing fields and a consensus may not exist on every point. Many of the current theories are highly mathematical in nature rather than physical. Science advances in several different ways. One is mental, relying on reasoning and thought. This includes things like Aristotle's theories, general relativity, Maxwell's equations, parts of quantum physics, etc. Then experiments are designed and executed to verify them. Another is to observe phenomena and construct a theory to explain it. This is the basis of Newton's laws of motion. The third way would be combination of the first two. Then there is the method used by naturalists in merely observing behavior and recording it. In some cases it is impossible to devise experiments for verification of theories. These include one-of-a-kind-events such as the Big Bang. Even if an experiment is conducted that produces the desired result, it does not necessarily prove that it is the way it occurred. It may have been some other unknown process. Another reason, particularly in quantum and particle physics, the experimental facilities are not practical due to cost, size, or requiring a prohibiting amount of energy (like all the energy in the universe).

For many disciplines, physical laws were worked out based on how objects behaved. Mathematical formulations were devised from empirical data. Newton's laws of motion are an example. With the development of steam engines, laws of thermodynamics were discovered. The first law is that, in a closed system, energy remains constant; it is neither created nor destroyed. It may, however, change form (Einstein showed the equivalence between energy and matter). The second law of thermodynamics is that the total entropy of the universe is always increasing. Entropy is a coined engineering term used to measure the efficiency of engines. It is sometimes loosely referred to as a measure of disorder. More about it is given in the Appendix.

It is only much later that the theories were worked out for many of these laws; even though engineers became very adept at their use and many things were invented. The process usually involved a lot of trial and error. Thomas Edison was a master of the experimental technique. Most of the laws were proportional in nature. For example, the law of gravity states that the force of gravity between any two material objects in proportional to the product of their masses divided by the square of the distance between them. To make it an exact equation, a constant had to be introduced. The value of the constant depends on the measurement system (see the Appendix on measurement). But the "constant" remains constant for all time and in all places. The gravitational constant is only one of several "constants of nature." Some others will be introduced in later chapters. (See reference 11 for a very comprehensive discussion).

3

It's about Time

BECAUSE A LOT OF DISCUSSION is raised about the timeline in Genesis, I think it is important to understand what it is we are talking about when we talk about time. Although we deal with time and are often slaves to it, it is actually not a simple concept, and the obsession with it is recent. Try your own definition of time. Clocks were not invented until the 1300s and have been developed over centuries. A clock is a device for keeping track of time and may be measuring it in some sense. But exactly what is being measured? Perhaps the easiest thing to visualize is a "day." It is a period of light followed by a period of darkness (or the other way around). The duration of the periods is not the same (except twice a year at the equinoxes), the ratio varies during the year, and they do not appear simultaneously alike over the whole earth. A day is defined as the complete cycle of light and darkness, as from a high noon to the next high noon (high noon is when the sun has reached its highest point in the sky and when shadows are the shortest). This phenomenon is caused by three things: the earth's rotation so that a different part of it faces the sun, the axis of rotation of the earth is tilted with respect to a line from earth to sun, and the earth is orbiting the sun. A year is the period for the earth to do a complete orbit around the sun, which is not an even number of days; hence the need for a leap year. The seasons occur because of the position on the orbit and the tilt of the axis. The position on the orbit, and hence when an orbit is completed, can be determined by careful observation of the stars. The orbital velocity of the earth is slowing down and the radius of the orbit is decreasing. These two effects are so small as to not be observed except by careful, precise measurements; however, a leap second has to be added to the year occasionally.

A lunar month is the period for the moon to go through a complete cycle of its phases. The number of lunar months in a year is not a whole number; it is slightly more than 12. Our current months are given an arbitrary number of days and assigned 12 to a year. An extra day gets added to February in leap years to keep months and years aligned. The origin of the week is more obscure. Some cultures had different number of days in week. The ancient Egyptians favored a 10 day week and some people tried to adopt a ten day week during calendar reforms around the time of the French Revolution of the late 1700's. The Romans settled on a seven-day week, with each day named after the god who governed that day. For us, seven days is the obvious choice because of Genesis 1.

The definition of hours, minutes, and seconds is more obscure. One theory is that the Egyptians, in observing the apparent motion of the stars across the sky at night, saw 12 different constellations rise. They divided the night into 12 periods corresponding to the rise of each constellation. (The periods would probably not be equal, but so what?) Logically, then, the day was also thought of as 12 periods without having a good phenomenon to gauge it by except the position of the sun. I don't know how the 60 minutes and 60 seconds came about (there were some cultures that used a number-system base of 60 instead of 10). The point is that time periods are assigned according to observations by observers on earth. There is nothing intrinsic about the periods as far as the rest of the universe is concerned.

Archeologists have determined that many cultures devised ways of time keeping. It is thought that structures such as Stonehenge served as calendars. Examples are also seen in structures of the Aztecs, Mayans, and other American tribes. Whether they had finer time divisions is not certain. An early example of keeping time of finer divisions is the water clock used by the Egyptians and others. A container filled with water drained from a small orifice. If the flow remained fairly constant, the water level would be related to time. Inaccuracies arose from erosion of the orifice or mineral deposits. What we know as an hourglass, using sand instead of water, soon followed with the time period depending on the size of the container, the size of the grains of sand, and the size of the opening between the two halves. Someone had to remember to fill the water container or turn the glass over at the proper time.

There seem to be natural clocks built into living things. Some of these may be controlled by varying external conditions or built into the DNA. Animals and humans have a natural rhythm called the circadian rhythm. Hibernating animals know when to put on extra weight. Seeds sprout and plants bloom at specific times. Trees lose their leaves in the fall and grow back in the spring.

From the above discussion, we see that what we think of as time is very much an earth and human centered thing; it depends very much on the current configuration of the solar system and the universe as viewed from earth. Anywhere else in the universe such reference points would be meaningless. At the time of creation (from Genesis or the Big Bang) until the solar system had settled down, our way of measuring time did not exist. There is no requirement to assume God made everything appear at once as it is now. The current theories, most notably the Big Bang and Relativity, postulate that at the instant of creation everything emerged from a singularity; this includes matter, space, and time. The singularity would have zero size, infinite density, and infinite temperature. (See reference 1.)

During the early stages of the Big Bang, the laws of physics may not have worked in the same way as they do now. Time itself may have moved at a different rate, so it is not productive to apply our current observation of time to that period. A simplified description of the formation of the universe will show that our perception time is only an abstraction until the earth is finally formed. The scientific description of its forming is as follows:

The instant of the Big Bang or initial creation was a burst of a huge amount of energy. The energy condensed into particles as it cooled. (This will be a way too simple explanation; see any current text or book on cosmology such as reference 1 or reference 21 for a more detailed explanation.) Temperature is a measurement of the energy of particles (hence, their movement). The initial particles would be mainly electrons, photons, and neutrinos with a few protons and neutrons. As the universe expanded it would also cool off (motions decrease). This allowed the particles under the action of the weak and strong nuclear forces to form atoms. The first atoms would be the simplest, namely hydrogen with a nucleus of only one proton and one orbiting electron. As space expanded, the matter would be carried along with it. Under the influence of gravity, the atoms would be attracted to each other. As the mass of a particular lump of matter increased, pressure and temperature would be enough to fuse the hydrogen into helium. The process would continue to produce the heavier elements. Eventually gravity caused more and more particles to form larger masses. One may think of this as a condensation process. The larger masses would form the stars. Depending on the nature of the forces, planets and smaller masses would be formed and captured by the stronger gravity of the star. The centrifugal force would maintain the orbital distance. In truth, most planets are gradually spiraling into the stars. Stars that become massive enough continue to collapse into themselves. They become denser and hotter, and the heat and pressure drive fusion to produces heavier elements. Eventually the internal energy of the star becomes enough that it explodes as a super nova. The atoms are scattered in the universe where they can begin the process again. This time there will be heavy elements. Our solar system is estimated to be about 5 billion years old while the universe is now estimated at 14 billion years. This means the sun is a second or third generation star. The planets, including earth, formed about the same time as the sun. They would start out very hot. The inner four planets are solid while the outer ones are gaseous.

It is interesting how time is a factor in so many scientific theories and calculations. Perhaps the most famous and quoted equation (although the equation is not really understood) is Einstein's $E=mc^2$. In this case m is the mass of matter and c is the speed of light given in units of distance per unit of time. Why does time enter into this equation? Is it simply an artifact of our mathematics and terrestrial thinking? In the early phases of creation, our current laws of physics and certainly our measure of time would not have been valid. In the special theory of relativity, time is not a constant but is different for an observer at a fixed point and for one moving with respect to the fixed point (the difference only becomes significant as the moving observer's speed approaches the speed of light).

We use expressions in every day talk as if time were a commodity. We really can't do the things we say, like take time, have time, lose time, gain time, save time, waste time. Lamentations tells us how there is a time for everything.

Time is very much a human concept. Apparently no other creature has the sense of time that we do. Our time reckonings are all based on the motion of the earth and astronomical observations. The day and the year are the easiest to delineate. The only certain time during the day is high noon when the sun is at its zenith. All others are arbitrary. Hours were the first finer division; minutes and seconds came much later.

Anything like accurate time keeping did not occur until the 1300s when the first primitive (and highly inaccurate, large, and expensive) clocks were invented. The impetuous was from churches so that the members would know when to perform their required prayers; hence, why most clocks were located in church steeples. Islamic communities still use calls to prayers at specified times. Towns and cities installed clocks as a matter of prestige. Each locality had its own time based on the local high noon. This did not matter much when there were few portable clocks and travel was slow. The railroads changed all that because travel was finally fast enough to notice the differences. Standard time and time zones were not established until a world conference in 1884 agreed on the details. Railroads were very influential in determining the boundaries of time zones, especially in North America. Essentially in the larger universe, earth time means nothing.

All of this discussion about time is to show that trying to impose our conception of time on the early part of creation is not possible, whether from the scientific or biblical standpoint. Up until the creation of humans, there were no observers to even care about it. God is not limited to the view of time that we have. Even during most of the activities in the first 25 verses of Genesis, a human observer was lacking. What really is important is the relation to our lifespan. There is no anchor for establishing anything like numbering the years as we do now. We notice in the Bible that years are identified as being in the reign of a certain king. The contemporary cultures did the same thing. The first universally accepted calendar was created about the time of the life of Julius Caesar around 46 BC. During the 1570s the calendar was revised to what we use today. Its concern was due to the drifting date of the spring equinox and setting the date for Easter. It took a while for all countries to accept, especially in protestant (1700s), Eastern Orthodox (1923) countries, and China (1912, although they still have their own calendar and new year). Corrections have to be made to keep all the various time divisions synchronized. That is why we have such things as leap years. In the early 1700s there was an adjustment of several days, so we cannot be too adamant in setting dates.

4

A Quick Look
at the Seven

EVERYTHING MATERIAL HAS BEEN CREATED by the end of Genesis 1:2. At first the earth was not fit for human habitation. It is not clear (at least to me) what is implied by the statement "the Spirit of God was moving over the face of the waters." This could very well mean that some changes were taking place. Nothing in these first two verses can be used to indicate the time involved. In fact, as we saw in the last chapter, in the early days of the universe, time was not the same as we think of it today. There were no human observers, and the celestial motions that we use to mark time were not fully settled down. God was not through with creation.

Before looking specifically at the six days of creation (seven, if you want to include the rest day), a few general things need to be noted. Genesis was written to the Israelites (probably at Sinai) who had just come out of Egypt after 400 years. Even though they had been in their own community, they were still steeped in Egyptian culture and beliefs. The Egyptians had a god for everything. The six days shows that these gods are false, that the creation was by the one God of Israel and things work according to His design, not through the control of some god. The earth is being prepared for humans and functions of the created elements are being assigned. That is, the things that have already been created materially are now being given their function.

There are many theories about the actual period of time in each of the days. As I stated earlier, on one hand I believe all of them, and on the other hand, I don't believe any of them. I believe that people think they have good reasons for believing what they do, but they are missing the whole point and focus of the account. It is God who has done this and it is for our benefit. The details that we quibble about are irrelevant. It is about the who, not the what. In sticking to the idea of considering how the Israelites would have thought about it, the days would have been a period of darkness followed by a period of light (sunset to sunset; why this order I don't know) or sunrise to sunrise as we view it. However, all the material objects are in place and only the functions are being assigned. Our hypothetical Israelite would have had no interest in the material universe but only the gods involved, how they run things, and how they can be appeased. But for the Israelites the whole cosmos becomes the temple of their God (Isa. 66:1–2). After the material is created it needs to be made functional. If the universe is 14 billion years old, so be it. If the earth is 5 billion years old, so be it. This is not what is being described in the six days. If we were to insist on six literal days, why did it take six days? It could have been done all at once in an instant. Also the days are described by saying "there was evening and there was morning"; this would only be 12 hours and it would be at night! But by describing a progression of the appearance of the features of earth necessary for human existence, order is maintained and the significance of humans is established. Thus the six days only mark the end of a phase of creation.

One way to view the days as normal 24-hour days is to not require the seven days to be consecutive; rather that they mark the end of a period of creativity and in which the functions are assigned. We use the idea of giving certain days names (for example, New Years' Day, Christmas Day, Valentine's Day, Labor Day, etc.). Just because the days in Gen. 1 are identified by a number does not mean they were consecutive. We use the term "Independence Day" and celebrate each year, but independence did not really occur on that particular day, as it was only the day when the Declaration of Independence was signed. A lot work had been done leading up to that day to produce the document, and a war still had to be fought. We also remember "D-day," the day in June

1944 when the allied forces invaded Normandy, which eventually led to the end of World War II. In this case also, a lot of work had gone into the preparation, getting forces and equipment in place, and planning the attack. Likewise in creation, we can talk of certain days of creation without meaning that everything was completed on that particular day or that the entire task was completed. This would explain the use of the phrase "there was evening and there was morning" for Days 1–6 but not for Day 7. This is not the same as the "age-day" concept. Thus we can still consider that a day means a day as the Israelites would have understood it and yet realize that creation proceeded over a long time.

After verse 1:1, the Hebrew word for create (bara) is not used again until verses 1:21, 27. In the English translations, the phrase "let there be" is used in verses 1:3, 6, and 14; the word "let" is used in verses 1:9 (2 times), 11, 14, 15, 20 (2 times), 24, and 26 (2 times). Concordances that index according to the Hebrew words do not reference these verses under "let." ("Let" first appears in Ex. 3:19 with meaning "allow.") This means the usages here were from other Hebrew expressions or were added by the translators. All of the versions I checked had these words except for The Message. If these words are not really there, the English can be misleading, implying that something new is made. However, without those words, it implies that something is being used that is already there. I favor the later as create in this context can have the meaning of assigning a function (John Walton introduces the idea of assigning functions in reference 15; I have not seen the concept any-where else); therefore, the day could be our normal day without saying anything about the age of the universe or earth. I think examining the activities of each day carefully lends credence to this view.

The events of Exodus 32:1–6 must have been very discouraging to Moses. All of his effort (the Ten Commandments have been given) and still the people turn to other gods. This is probably why Genesis was written. Chapter 1 is making it clear that the Egyptian gods are not responsible creation; it is the one God of Israel. To relate the seven days to the Egyptian culture, I include some Egyptian deities that might be associated with the things being created. These are a composite from several web sites. Other time functions easily follow. No material thing is necessarily created in these verses; it deals with what already exists.

In the following discussion I will use the term "Day X" as a short-hand to indicate all the activity occurring before the actual designated day on which the functions are assigned regardless of the time that was required.

Day 1 establishes the role of alternating light and darkness. Visible light is a very small part of the entire spectrum of electromagnetic waves. We had noted earlier that the waves we are used to are waving something, so the idea of an aether was proposed. An unknown medium to wave was left after the aether was proven not to exist. If a vacuum contains nothing, how can a wave propagate through it? Waves do not need something moving at the same velocity as the wave itself. Throw a stone in a pond and waves propagate from the point of impact. The water is not moving, only the action. The best example of how this works is the recent fad of the audience wave in a stadium. It is accomplished by people standing up and sitting down in sequence. The people themselves do not move but the wave does. The current theory is that what is waving in electromagnetic radiation is space itself. It is believed that similar gravity waves exist, which have a very long wavelength. (Experimental verification is still being sought.) The primary thing that exists is darkness, which is the absence of light. Light is not a material thing, but is energy. This may be why the days are delineated by giving the evening first and then the morning. Thus you cannot have a mixture of light and darkness that is separated like, say, oil and water. You do not see light itself except as it is emitted from a source or when it strikes an object. The light that we see during the day is due to the scattering of the light by the atmosphere. If you go above the atmosphere (or shield the light or have no atmosphere), the sky is dark. Alternating periods of darkness followed by light gives a method of keeping time. It does not matter that the sun is not mentioned until Day 4 where it is also given other functions because there are lots of other light sources in the universe. (After all, cosmologists set the creation of the universe at 14 billion years ago and the creation of the solar system at 5 billion years ago.) Other time functions easily follow. No material thing is created in this verse; it deals with what already exists. The Egyptian gods are Khepera, god of the rising sun and Atum, god of the setting sun.

Day 2 is the separating of the waters. Cosmology of the time had a layer of upper waters and a layer of lower waters. If rain came down, the water must be above and something must hold it back. They called this barrier the firmament. God does not at this point explain how the rain cycle actually works. Water evaporates from the oceans, and the vapor rises in the atmosphere and condenses into clouds; the drops become heavy enough to fall and the water collects in rivers that drain it back into the ocean and cycle starts again. God uses the current cosmology and points out He is responsible for it. The waters were already mentioned as being created in verse 1:2, so no new material thing is created here. The separating here provided a living space in between for us. Rain is not given until verses 2:5–6. The Egyptian gods are Nun, god of the primordial waters and Tefnut, goddess of moisture and rain.

Day 3 involves a couple of things. Dry land and water are separated. People living in Egypt would understand this concept. Before the Aswan dam was built, every year the Nile River would flood lower Egypt. As the flood waters receded, a layer of silt was left behind (which actually provided a new layer of rich soil). The dry land and the waters were separated. Next, vegetation began (or continued) its cycle. Here the text does not say that God made it but the land "brought forth." We know that vegetation requires light that was already functioning from Day 1. Requisite amount of light now comes to the earth from the sun. See also verses 2:4b–6. The Egyptian gods are Geb, god of the earth; Anqet, water goddess; Hapi, god of the Nile; Khnemu, god of the Nile inundation; Satet, goddess of the Nile and fertility; Renenutet, goddess of the harvest.

The first three days we saw the functions set up. In the next three days the focus shifts to the objects providing those functions. There is a parallel between Days 1 and 4, Days 2 and 5, and Days 3 and 6.

Day 4 further describes the functions of the sources of light from Day 1. The lights in Genesis 1:14 are recognized as sun, moon, and stars. In accommodating the cosmology of the times, they are placed in the firmament. Besides giving light, they are to provide further ways of keeping time. Because of the latitude of Egypt, the seasons mentioned are probably not winter, summer, etc. as we know them but more likely sowing and harvest. Verse 1:16 is an elaboration of Genesis 1:14 so is dealing with existing items. There is no attempt in this verse to explain how the rotation of the earth causes day and night or how the earth orbiting the sun causes seasons; that is left for Copernicus to discover. The functions are human oriented; not scientifically oriented. Along with Day 3, the basis for food established. Egyptian gods are Re, creator god of the sun; Aten, disk of the sun; Khonsu, Theban god of the moon; Aker, guardian of the traveling sun; Horus, falcon-god of the sun; Sopdet, goddess of the star "Sirius"; Thoth, Ibis-god of wisdom and the moon.

Day 5 adds functions to the waters of Day 2. Verse 1:20 opens with "the waters bring forth . . ." and so there were "swarms" of creatures in the sea. This is what the seas were made to do. This does not conflict with the fact that some sea life existed prior to the land teeming with plant life in Day 3; rather, the sea life greatly expands. Verse 1:21 seems to be a slight expansion of verse 20. It is past tense in that this is what God has done. It is unsure what the "great sea monsters" are, but probably things like whales, sharks, and other large fish. The birds are also identified in this verse. Egyptian gods are Sobek, god of the crocodiles; Heket, frog goddess of infinity.

Day 6 finishes the creative activity with populating the land with animals and eventually humans. Similar to verse 1:20, verse 1:24 begins "the earth bring forth . . ." after their kinds. Were the kinds already there? Likewise verse 1:25 seems an expansion of verse 24. The end of verse 25, "And God saw that it was good . . ." signals the end of this phase of creation; that is, the earth is now prepared for human habitation. Everything is established and working as it was designed to do. Egyptian gods are Baal, Semitic god of storms; Bastet, cat goddess of the home; Nut, goddess of the sky; Shu, god of the air; and others.

I hope that by including the Egyptian gods it becomes clear why creation had to be explained as it is in Genesis 1. There were a lot of gods and a lot of myths that had to be dispelled. We may now also see why weaning the Israelites off idols took so long and why they so easily asked for and accepted the molten calf in Exodus 32.

Humans don't appear until Gen. 1:26. (One point from Hebrew lexicons is that adam is a Hebrew word frequently meaning man in the generic sense.) The plural form is used here, indicating that there were multiple beings. Verse 27 even emphasizes that there were male and female. Nothing so far requires that only a single human was created. It is only with the planting of the Garden of Eden that an individual is singled out. Our biases have propagated the idea that the garden was planted for the benefit of Adam and Eve. This is not the case.

The garden was to be the sacred space where God would appear. It was not intended to be a paradise for people (even though it would have been). Thus Genesis 3:8 talks about God moving about the garden; that is why He planted it. It was a place where God could come to earth and interact with people. (We see similar concepts throughout the Bible.) It is seen in Genesis 2:15, that man was to work in the garden, to tend, till, and keep it. As a reward for his efforts, man was allowed the benefits of the garden except for the fruit of the tree of knowledge. Eve was formed from Adam's side to be his helper. There is nothing to imply that they were the only humans, only that they were selected for a special task; that of tending to God's sacred space and as a result being the go-between for humans and God. From this point on the Bible then focuses on specific individuals and peoples to carry out the work of God.

With the view of Genesis 1–3 presented so far we can trace the work through the rest of the Bible. There is now no problem about the source of Cain's wife. She simply came from those humans who were not selected to care for the Garden of Eden. From the time of Adam and Eve's sin, no human is allowed to enter the garden because of the tree of life and the wickedness of humans outside the garden continued to increase. Few were righteous before God. Finally, by chapter 6, God was sorry He had made humans and determined to blot them out; however, Noah was found to be righteous, and he and his family were to be spared. Whether the flood was limited in scope or universal is immaterial. Wickedness was dealt with. The Bible focuses only on the individuals important to the story. Noah's emergence from the ark gave rise to another type of (limited) sacred space for God; that of the altar in Gen. 8:20.

The idea of a sacred space where people could meet with their gods was very common in the cultures of this time. Spaces were built and the gods were begged to come down to them. It is often thought that the tower of Babel was conceived as a way for humans to ascend to heaven, but it was more likely intended as a way for God to descend to earth. Perhaps that is why the pyramids in Egypt were built, to allow the gods to come down and dwell with the deceased Pharaoh. Other examples from the Bible would include the holy of holies in the tabernacle and in the temple. That would explain why the destruction of the temple was so devastating to the Israelites; they no longer had a place to meet with God. In the New Testament, our bodies are now called the temple of God because He dwells in us.

The question is often raised as to where the dinosaurs and similar prehistoric creatures fit in. The answer is that they don't. The discovery of such fossils has only been in the last 200 years or so. The people at the time Genesis was written had no knowledge of them so there would be no reason to mention them. The paleontology evidence shows that the extinction of the dinosaurs occurred long before humans were created. There is absolutely no conflict between Gen. 1 and the paleontology record because there is no overlap in the time covered by each. There were at least two mass extinctions in the record in which almost all species were wiped out. These happened before the events described in the days of creation that tell of assigning functions to the created material of Genesis 1:1–2. This discussion is expanded in the Appendix.

The creation of humans and the seventh day (day of rest) will be treated in the next chapter. In taking the view of an Israelite at the time of writing, they most likely viewed the idea of a day as being from sunset to sunset. I believe that all the material part of creation is done by the end of Genesis 1:2. The creative activity described in each of the paragraphs of Gen. 1 ends in a numbered day. John Walton (see reference 15) says the purpose of the special days is to assign functions and get things going. There is nothing in the days relating to the age of the earth or universe. I have a book published in 1988, one in 2002, and one in 2016. The age of the universe has gone from 6 billion years to 10 billion to 14 billion. The age of the earth itself varies from 2 to 5 billion years. The detailed accounts in Genesis occur so recently that these ages are of no import.

In all my studies of Genesis before, I considered the account very straight forward. As I got into it deeper, I discovered I did not really know what I thought I did. I found a lot of things were not quite like I thought they were and there was a lot more to it than I had imagined. Besides, I got interested or renewed my interest in several of the tangents. That is still going on. Particularly, I realized how important the background was and how many assumptions I had made about things weren't quite right or complete. We may not cover everything in each of the first three chapters, but, overall, I won't leave much out. With the current state of affairs in the world, I believe that morality is at a low. I blame a good part of this on the attacks on religion in general and Christianity in particular because that eliminates any standard or higher authority. With this book I hope to remove some of the objections that have been used from these three chapters to cast doubt on the veracity of the Bible. We seem to me to be a state similar to that in Judges 17:6 and 21:25 that "every man did what was right in his own eyes" (RSV).

I spent a lot of time talking about Egypt (dating 3,500 years ago). The question of "what does that have to do with Genesis 1–3?" might be raised. The answer is: everything. The Israelites had been there for 400 years and it becomes obvious that they had been influenced by the experience. I think we cannot understand what was happening in Exodus without having the information in Genesis (hence, why it was written). I also believe that we cannot really understand Genesis without knowing Exodus and beyond. The goal of both for us is the same: appreciate what God has done for us and how great He is. There are no other gods before Him.

There are at least two candidates for the molten calf god (Ex. 32) that Aaron made: Bat, ancient celestial cow goddess; and Hathor, cow goddess of love and music.

5

Creation Climax

WONDERING ABOUT WHAT IS GOING on in the six days (and before) when there were no human observers is like asking the well-known question, "If a tree falls in the forest and no one is around to hear it, does it still make a sound?" The answer is, of course, yes and no. The falling tree will create the variations in air pressure that form into sound waves. (It does this all the way to the ground; why is it intensified when it hits the ground?) However, the air pressure waves have no meaning until they stimulate the receptors in an ear, and they still need to be converted to nerve impulses and transmitted to the brain and interpreted by it. Only then do we call it a sound even though the events leading up to it are been going on in the meantime.

In a similar way the question could be asked, "If all the things in Genesis 1 are made but there is no observer present, are they really created?" Because in the way they are described, they are tailored to support human life. This is a view held by many cosmologists, even if they are not religious. They came up with the anthropic principle, independently of theologians, which we will discuss in the next chapter. In the same way as the falling tree, creation could not be considered done until everything was in place, given its function, and the humans created who could sense and appreciate it.

The tailoring of the universe for humans would lead us to wonder if in the vastness of the universe, are there others like us? My own opinion is we may never know. The time required for the travel is too great. Others could have existed on distant planets but by the time we would find them, they would be extinct. People who think about such things have estimated that the duration of a civilization is about 10,000 years before they use up all their resources or kill each other off, although they could have sent a message into space that would reach us long after they ceased to exist. We have sent just such messages. Ancient civilizations have been found that existed in the last few thousand years that lasted a far shorter time than 10,000 years. If God created other beings in other parts of the universe, Genesis doesn't tell us about them nor exclude them.

The climax of creation begins with Genesis 1:26b. There are really three parts to it. The first part is that God describes Himself in the plural. Many ideas have been expressed about the use of the plural. We can look elsewhere for a solution in places that would not have been available to the Israelites at Sinai. The Spirit of God has been introduced in Genesis 1:2 with no identification. Many passages in the New Testament tell us that Christ was involved, or at least present at the time of creation; John 1:1–3; Hebrews 1:2, for example. At this point no other heavenly beings have been mentioned. The first mention of an angel is in Genesis 16:7. However, it would seem that the Israelites knew about them and other beings such as cherubs as used in the tabernacle and temple (Ezek. refers a lot to cherubs). The Hebrew word for angel is malak and the Greek word is aggelos. In both languages the meaning is messenger or agent. There is no mention of them being created nor of them having a role in creation. Thus Genesis 1–3 is only concerned with humans; preparing the earth for them and creating them and so does not talk about other beings. Just because something is said to happen because God spoke it does not mean that it happened instantaneously. God told Abraham that he would have a son. It was 12 years before it happened and Sarah caused trouble by being impatient. He also promised Abraham that he would be the start of a great nation; it didn't happen until centuries later with the conquest of Canaan. "The Lord is not slow about His promise . . ." in 2 Peter 3:9 (RSV).

Humans appear in the second part. The last part of Day 6 in Gen. 1:26 states that man (humans) was "made" in God's image and "created" as male and female in verse 27. The use of the plural indicates that there were more than one or two individuals. (Ironically, the text that most convinces me of this is the same one that is used to prove that Adam was the first and only man created. This is 1 Cor. 15:42–50, which will be examined in more detail in a later chapter). The Hebrew word for man is "adam," which is sometimes used with a definite article and sometimes not. How it is translated depends on whether the definite article is used with it and the bias of the translators. For example, it is not used as a proper name until Genesis 3:17 in the Revised Standard Version and other translations. Walton (reference 14, page 42) points out that being created in the image of God can be understood in a least four categories: the role and function that God has given humans, the identity humans are given (distinct from animals), a substitute representing His presence on earth, and indicating the relationship He intends to have with humans (Col. 3:10, Jas. 3:9).

From passages such as Isaiah 66:1 and others that express similar sentiments, we see that the Israelites considered the whole universe to be the temple where God lived. (Remember that they had a much more restricted view of the universe than we do.) They also thought of the earth as being the center of that universe. A temple, being the place where a god lived, was where his image was kept (numerous examples of this in the OT). Humans, then, as the image of God are placed in the center of His temple, the earth. In other words, we are God's image in His temple.

The functions or work of humans is given just prior to their creation in 1:26 and told to them in 1:28. They were given dominion over all the other living things (see also Ps. 8:6–8). Verse 1:28 instructs them to fill the earth and subdue it. This is a broad command and we can speculate about what it entails. I say that it means, in part, that not every detail about the earth is given to them but they must find out some things for themselves. We are given the capability to study the creation and how it works as well as how to care for it. Curiosity is as much of a human trait as it is of cats. Every plant-yielding seed and every tree-bearing seed in its fruit were given as food for both humans and animals. The seed reference is why some people do not eat mushrooms or ferns, for instance. Does this mean we should not eat seedless grapes, tangerines, watermelon, and other things like that? What about poisonous plants? Thus Day 6 ends.

A thorough review of the claims by anthropologists and others about human origins is beyond the scope of this study, but I will talk about a few things in later chapters. A few comments are in order. There is a class of scientific disciplines that are deductive in nature. They study relics, artifacts, and conditions from the past and try to deduce the history behind them. Among this class are geology, anthropology, archeology, paleontology, parts of biology, and similar fields. In dealing with the past, there is no way to do comprehensive, controlled experiments. The work is painstaking, slow, and requires a lot of patience and attention to detail (and money). Experiments that are conducted have no assurance of duplicating past events or conditions. Most of the work is perceived by people in general as having no direct benefit to the present. A few exceptions exist such as how geology relates to petroleum exploration and biology to pharmacology. So how do they get funding? Most are university professors. Most operate from grants, gifts, and the like. There is a lot of competition, which at times, has even been violent, for the available funds. Those providing the funding expect results. A researcher may be tempted to exaggerate, report prematurely, or at worst, fake results to preserve or renew funding. A large theory may be constructed from a small, incomplete artifact.

A further note on the evolution controversy may help to deal with it. Although there are questions about the power of the survival of the fittest (the evolutionists like to use the euphemism, "natural selection") and about whether it really happens, the attitude and world view of the adherents is what really fuels the controversy. First is the belief in the power of the human mind to understand everything correctly. Evolutionists have unbridled faith in their abilities. They and other people (especially skeptics) assume that a theory they believe in can be applied to a much broader area than what it really addresses. This happened when Isaac Newton came up with his laws of physics. Some scientists seemed to think that because the laws worked well in a set of cases, those laws could be used to solve all sorts of things. Such things as social behavior were considered as fair game for the laws. (If only the initial conditions were known, future events would be determined by application of Newton's laws.) Of course, that turned out not to be the case. With the development of quantum theory, the uncertainty principle, and the theory of relativity, Newton's laws were limited in scope. The lesson evidently was not learned. The evolutionist of the late 1800s believed they'd been given a key to understanding far more than origin of the species. They saw evolution as applying to history, society, economics, to God, the cosmos, language and logic, and to the mind itself. In 1887 Thomas Huxley believed that applied evolutionary theory would deliver a unified explanation of everything: biology, physics, chemistry, and religion.

Today there is a school of thought that denies non-math and non-physics truths, and has been named physicalism. It is faith based and has all the trappings of a religion. But there are other issues that are not in the realm of physics. What does the color blue look like and how would you explain it to a person blind from birth? The evidence leads to the conclusion that physics is incomplete, that it will never be capable of describing all of reality. Science cannot address even the most essential aspects of the world, such as the flow of time and the meaning of now. Physicalists believe for something to exist, you must be able to measure it.

As we saw in chapter 3, time is not an easy concept and it is thought that, of all creatures, only humans have a sense of time. You don't really have time or need time, as time will continue regardless of what you do. Even our apportioning and categorizing is recent. Until 1884 there was no such thing as worldwide time zones or standard times (around 1850, England managed to establish a standard time for the whole country). In the US in the mid-1880s there were at least 144 official time zones. The confusion was tremendous. Railroads changed that. For the first time, travel was fast enough that the time differences could be noticed. Worldwide time zones were not established until the Prime Meridian Conference was held in Washington, DC, in 1884. This was the work of a Canadian named Sandford Fleming (reference 16).

The plan for the rest of this book is to study chapters 2 and 3 for however many chapters are needed then to look at the current state of a few topics that relate to creation in the Appendix. Topics include cosmology, evolution, relativity, geology (such as ice ages and tectonic plates), more on the concept of time, and quantum theory. The discussion will be limited due to lack of space and knowledge; however, one topic is so interesting, controversial, and significant that it will be studied in the whole next chapter.

6

The Anthropic Principle

IT WILL TAKE A WHILE but eventually I will get to how all of this is related to Genesis chapter 1.

The origin of the universe and the nature of it began to intrigue thinkers once people had the leisure to think about such things. As more was learned, there was more to be learned. As noted earlier, the first method was to propose a multitude of gods that made things, controlled things, and even were embodied in things seen around us, but the God of the Bible is unique. He created the material universe, established laws to govern the behavior of the material universe, and created humans to have dominion over all of the earth (and maybe the entire universe). Humans were given minds capable of studying creation in detail and discovering the laws of operation. Thus scientific endeavors could be undertaken because the universe was orderly. Many skeptics (and believers) do not appreciate how the Bible freed inquiry from the chains imposed by having capricious gods and being subject to their whims.

Logically, the first question to ask is "Where did it all come from?" Science was now free to search for the mechanisms of how it happened. Until very recently, those who did not accept religious sources of the origin could not propose a beginning. They thought that the universe had simply always existed as it is and would continue to do so. This avoided any need to explain a beginning because there was none. As techniques and instruments improved the universe could be better understood. Copernicus shook things up with the idea that the earth was not the center of the solar system but that it orbited around the sun. Galileo helped firmly establish this concept and studied orbits of other bodies. Isaac Newton worked out mechanical laws that were able to predict planetary motion (among other things). The prevailing theory became that of a steady state universe in that no substantial changes were taking place.

Around 1900, several scientific developments occurred. The atomic theory of matter was not fully accepted and the processes that powered the sun and stars were unknown. As often happens in science, two seemingly wide disparate fields were informing another. In 1905 Albert Einstein published a paper that eventually won him the Nobel Prize, even though it is not the theory he is most famous for. (He is famous for very many and significant innovations of the twentieth century.) His published paper was a theory for the photo-electric effect. When certain materials were beamed with light, electrons would be emitted. Selenium is an element with such properties. Einstein's theory showed that the electrons were emitted only with discrete energies. He proposed that the energy of an emitted electron was proportional to the wavelength (which determines its color) of the light. Increasing the light intensity produced more electrons but did not change the energy of the individual electrons. He also proposed that, in this case, the light behaved as a particle rather than a wave. In some cases light behaves as a wave (diffraction) and in other cases as a particle. The theory was proven mathematically and has been verified by numerous experiments and applications ever since. The particle of light was named a photon and the energy is given by the frequency times a constant (this constant had been found previously by Max Planck and is called "Planck's Constant"). The theory also showed that electrons could only occupy discrete energy levels or orbits in the atom.

Einstein's work opened the flood gates to other advances that came to be known as quantum mechanics and now known as quantum physics. Others developed the theory that every entity in particle physics can behave as either a particle or a wave. This forms the basis for today's electron microscopes where electron waves are used as the probe instead of visible light. The smaller wavelength of the electron made it possible to image smaller objects. It was certainly the final straw in establishing the validity of the theory, which Niels Bohr developed in 1912, with the structure of the atom being a nucleus with orbiting electrons (for which Bohr won the Nobel Prize). Bohr's theory was modified in 1916 to include elliptical orbits rather than circular ones. Later it was shown that the electrons could only occupy discrete energy levels or orbits. The number of electrons per orbit was discovered by Wolfgang Pauli to be limited to two (the Pauli exclusion principle). Chemical bonding is now explained by atoms sharing electrons. (There is much more to this story and it is continuing today. It is very fascinating when a 100 years' worth of work by dozens of people can be condensed down to a few pages, leaving out all the drudgery and frustration by those actually involved. There is a lot of high-level mathematics involved in the above theories.)

Now I will connect all of the above to cosmology. Quantum physics provides the fundamentals for nuclear reactions and the building of stars. A rough outline of the processes forming the universe are described below (the processes are still going on).

The concept of the universe once again saw a dramatic shift when Edwin Hubble discovered that the universe was expanding (circa. 1929). He explained it by the Big Bang theory, which is mentioned in other places in this book. Stephen Hawking gives an interesting description of the early beginning of the Big Bang in his book listed in the references (reference 1). The starting point is thought to have been a singularity: a point of infinite mass, density, temperature, and energy. Exactly what it was and how it started is unknowable from a scientific point of view. Any evidence would have been destroyed by the process. A theory of the beginning expansion is that it was very rapid and the laws of physics might have been different. This is called an inflationary period. As the expansion continued, the temperature and density would have decreased. Cooling allowed matter to form governed by Einstein's equation of $E=mc^2$. The initial particles to form would be the smallest: electrons and protons. There would be nothing to favor whether the electron would have negative charge and the proton positive or the other way around, but it is thought that both types existed. An atom with a negative nucleus and a positive orbiting particle is called antimatter. An electron type particle with a positive charge was named a positron. Such particles have been produced in nuclear reactions. If matter and antimatter collide, they annihilate each other with a release of a tremendous amount of energy. (This was the fuel for the starship Enterprise in the Star Trek series.) The universe could have developed as either matter- or antimatter-based, but a sight bias toward the production of matter meant that it prevailed. (Some speculate that a parallel universe of antimatter was produced at the same time.) High temperature would keep the electrons and protons separated, but as the universe expanded, cooling could allow atoms to eventually be formed. The first atoms to form would consist of only one proton and one electron, hydrogen, which is the lightest element and the only naturally occurring one with no neutrons in the nucleus. The force of gravity would cause clusters of atoms to form. As these clusters became more dense and hotter, hydrogen atoms would fuse together to form an atom containing two protons and two electrons. This configuration is unstable but becomes stable with the addition of two neutrons, which is helium. The fusion occurs more readily if the hydrogen atoms contain a neutron. Such an isotope of hydrogen, called deuterium, exists naturally but is unstable. A third isotope that exists contains two neutrons but is even rarer and more unstable.

The process continues to produce stars as the hydrogen and helium are drawn together by gravity. Once the mass of the star becomes large enough, further fusion reactions can take place with the release of energy. To form carbon three helium atoms need to fuse together and four helium atoms need to fuse together to form oxygen. (There are, of course, intermediate steps.) Heavier elements are formed by the continuing process. As a star becomes very massive, internal energy reaches a level that causes the star to explode as a super nova. All of the matter is scattered as particles into space and the process is repeated to form larger bodies; large bodies of gas (hydrogen and helium) become stars again while the heavier elements condense into planets (some planets are also gaseous but not massive enough to become stars and are captured by a star), asteroids, and moons over billions of years. So we are now in the present configuration of the universe as it continues to expand at an accelerating rate. All of this is explained in Genesis in just two verses, Genesis 1:1–2.

As cosmologists and others contemplate the creation of the universe, some curious coincidences appear. For everything to work, certain parameters are confined to very close limits. Collectively these parameters are known as the constants of nature. We are familiar with constants from studies such as high school geometry. The Greek letter pi (π) is used to represent the ratio of the circumference of a circle to its diameter and is constant, regardless of the size of the circle. Other constants arise naturally in all of mathematics. For example, the base for natural logarithms designated by the letter "e" (e=1+ 1/1!+!/2!+1/3!+1/4!+1/5!+ . . . where n!=1x2x3x . . . n and to eight decimal places is 2.71828183). (Unless otherwise noted, e will be used as the smallest unit of electrical charge equal to the charge on the electron.) Another is "i" to represent the square root of -1. We will look at just a very few others, but first a little introduction to them:

From the dust jacket of The Constants of Nature by John D. Barrow, reference 11:

> The constants of nature are the numbers that define the universe. They tell us how strong its forces are and what its fundamental laws can do: the strength of gravity and magnetism, the speed of light, and the masses of the smallest particles. They encode the deepest secrets of the universe, and their existence tells us that nature abounds with unseen regularities. Yet while we have become adept at measuring the values of these constants, our inability to explain or predict them shows how much we still have to learn about the cosmos.

The electron mass/proton mass ratio is designated by the Greek letter beta. The value is approximately 1/1836: if it is much bigger, the electrons will not occupy their well-defined orbits around the nucleus, and there would be no ordered molecular structure. Another dimensionless constant associated with the atom is called the fine structure constant and is a measure of the strength of the electromagnetic force that governs how electrically charged elementary particles and photons interact. The value is approximately 1/137. For an atom to exist, there is a very narrow range of values that beta and the fine structure constant can have.

The volume of three-dimensional objects is roughly proportional the cube of their size and the mass will be proportional to the volume.

The density (mass divided by volume) of everything in the universe is roughly equal to the density of an atom (after all, everything is made up of atoms). This sets a limit on the strength of gravity that living things could endure. (Think about the results being obtained of the effect of weightlessness on people living for extended times on the International Space Station.)

There are many other constants that can have only a very restricted range of values and living organisms survive. Some of these are easily observed such as the speed of light while others are deep in exoteric physics equations. The pursuit of the understanding of the fundamental nature of matter and the forces of nature has led the positing of a large number (50 plus) of different particles. These fit into the theoretical equations and experimental results have verified predictions, although the particles may, in fact, be virtual. The wave characteristic of the particle may be the one used. This is too deep to continue further here.

The delicate balances of so many factors in the universe that make life possible has not escaped the attention of scientists. In 1959 Fred Hoyle wrote (cited in reference 11, page157):

> I do not believe that any scientists who examined the evidence would fail to draw the inference that the laws of nuclear physics have been deliberately designed with regard to the consequences they produce inside the stars. If this is so, then my apparently random quirks have become part of a deep-laden scheme. If not then we are back again at a monstrous sequence of accidents.

Regardless of what conclusions are reached or where faith is placed, the fact of this balance cannot be denied. A concise statement was coined to sum up this balance. Brandon Carter came up with the term anthropic principle in 1973. The term "principle" is used to denote a statement that most agree is true (like an axiom) but is not subject to proof as a theory is. Some would use the term "conjecture." Carter later regretted using the prefix "anthropic" because it specifically is used to refer to humans while the principle applies to all of life. It is still used because most understand the distinction and don't worry about it. The principle has been phrased in a number of different ways and has been separated into a weak and a strong version. I will list a number of them to give you a feel for the idea.

Brandon Carter's original version of the weak is "that what we can expect to observe must be restricted by the condition necessary for our presence as observers." His version of the strong is "that the Universe (and hence the fundamental parameters on which it depends) must be such as to admit the creation of observers within it at some stage." (Cited in reference 11, page162–164).

Freeman Dyson said (Freeman Dyson, Disturbing the Universe, Harper & Rowe. New York, 1979), "I do not feel like an alien in this universe. The more I examine the universe and study the details of its architecture, the more evidence I find that the universe in some sense must have known that we were coming."

Encyclopedia Britannica also explains:

> Anthropic principle, in cosmology, any consideration of the structure of the universe, the values of the constants of nature, or the laws of nature that has a bearing upon the existence of life. Clearly, humanity's very existence shows that the current structure of the universe and the values taken by the constants of nature permit life to exist. Indeed, it appears that many features of the universe that are necessary for the evolution and persistence of life are the results of unusual coincidences between values of the constants of nature . . .

From Stephen Hawking in 1988 (reference 1, page 124ff):

> The weak anthropic principle states that in a universe that is large or infinite in space and/or time, the conditions necessary for the development of intelligent life will be met only in certain regions that are limited in space and time. The intelligent beings in these regions should therefore not be surprised if they observe that their locality in the universe satisfies the conditions that are necessary for their existence
>
> [The strong version]: there are either many different universes or many different regions of a single universe, each with its own initial configuration and, perhaps, with its own set of laws of science. In most of these universes the conditions would not be right for the development of complicated organisms; only in the few universes that are like

ours would intelligent beings develop and ask the question;
"Why is the universe the way we see it?" Then answer is then
simple: if it had been different, we would not be here.

Merriam-Webster Dictionary's definition of anthropic principle is:

anthropic principle, *noun*
definition: either of two principles in cosmology
a: conditions that are observed in the universe must allow
the observer to exist
—called also *weak anthropic principle*
b: the universe must have properties that make inevitable
the existence of intelligent life
—called also *strong anthropic principle*

Many people do not find an anthropic principle useful because they
have to find some other explanation for the coincidences. Others latch
onto it as proof of a designer for the universe. I think both are missing
the point. It is useful and it does not need to prove anything. I would
consider it more from the concepts of formal logic as what would be
called necessary conditions but not sufficient conditions. They exist
and that is that. We live in a universe that is finely tuned for our existence. If there were even very small changes in certain conditions and
constants, we could not exist. These facts are true, but what we make
of them and how we use them depends our own biases, philosophies,
and beliefs.

7

Becoming Ready
for Humans

THERE IS A CHANGE OF focus beginning in verse 2:4 and is seen in the introductory phrase: "These are the generations of . . ." The phrase or its equivalent is used several times to introduce a new section in several Scripture verses: Genesis 2:4; 5:1; 6:9; 10:1; 11:10; 11:27; 25:12; 25:19; 36:1, 9; 37:2; Numbers 3:1; Ruth 4:18; and 1 Chronicles 1:29. Up until then the story has been about what we may refer to as the "big picture." From here on, it is the picture of the development of the nation of Israel, mainly through individuals, with its ultimate purpose of bringing Christ into the world. Some would put a large time gap between verses 2:3 and 2:4. There is nothing in the text that demands or excludes such a gap. It is irrelevant to the story being told; therefore, I will pause and give a recap of the story up to here and add a few related topics.

The writer of Genesis is universally believed to be Moses. Genesis was most likely written soon after the Exodus while the Israelites were camped at the base of Mt. Sinai. The reason for the writing was to answer the question Moses asked in Exodus 3:13 about the name of the God who is sending Moses. It is also to wean the Israelites away from the culture of polytheism. To understand Genesis, it is important to understand as much about the audience as possible. Any interpretation must be one that that audience would have understood and not base it upon our or any other world view and culture.

The Israelites as a people essentially begin with Abraham and have been living in Egypt for around 400 years, mostly as slaves. They are thoroughly steeped in the culture and religion of Egypt. They still worshipped Jehovah but accepted that there were other gods with some power. This view is based upon the fact that they so often turned to worship idols. The OT is full of examples of the Israelites being led astray. It was an important factor for Israel splitting into a northern and southern kingdom. At the height of idol worship is the story of Ahab and Jezebel. Polytheism was still prevalent in the NT, shown by Paul's visit to Athens in Acts 17. In a sense we still have a remnant of it today, as people consult their horoscope daily, or pray to patron saints.

The Israelites held the same view of the cosmos as others of the time: an underworld, a water layer as the source of wells and springs, the space where they lived, a layer of water as the source of rain held up by the firmament, and the heavenly bodies embedded in the firmament. If they thought about it all, they probably thought the earth was flat. There is no evidence that they had any interest in origins, material or otherwise. Most people of that era did not have the leisure for such pursuits because it took all their efforts just to survive. They had absolutely no knowledge of modern science or cosmologies. This study of Genesis 1 to 3 is to try as much as possible to understand it as they would have in their culture.

To emphasize, Genesis 1 to 3 was to be understood by the people living at the time and we should try to understand it from their perspective. They had not yet fully accepted the idea of only one God because they cared little for origins or anything else that did not contribute to their immediate survival. Therefore, Genesis has no indication or concern with the age of the universe or earth. It does not try to describe things in terms other than that which coincided with common belief about the material realm. It does not anticipate modern science, as science has changed much over history and is still changing, therefore such anticipation would make no sense. Genesis does proclaim the one God, Jehovah, and tell that He has made everything and put it into operation. All of this indicates His concern for us. The cosmos is not made up of many gods, but of objects created by Jehovah and set into operation by Him and sustained by Him. The cosmos is His dwelling place, a temple for Him.

In verses 1:1 and 2, the whole of the material universe is created. The Spirit of God moving over the earth must have had some purpose. Everything is made ready for the assigning of functions in verses 1:3–26. Absolutely no indication of the time involved is given nor details of things before verse three. The geological history of the earth and pre-historic creatures were unknown to people of the time so there would have been no reason to mention them. The starting point is with things that people observed and knew about. One of the tasks is to dispel the pagan myths that had grown up around the material world.

The Israelites would have considered the seven days as normal days. Because Genesis 1:1–2 describes the creation of the material part of the universe, the activity in the seven days says nothing about the age of the earth or universe. Functions are being assigned to the material in preparation for human habitation. Days 1 and 7 have no material component. Days 2, 3, 4, and 6 are dealing with material components already existing. Day 5 is not focused on new creation of material things. Day 7 is unique. There is no evening and morning as in the other days. The only mention of activity is the resting and the blessing and hallowing of the day. Speaking of the seven days as not having anything to do with the age of the earth in no way suggests that God did not make the universe and earth. In fact there many other passages in the Bible that say that He did (Col. 1:16–17; Heb. 1:2; 11:3); it's just that Genesis 1 is not that story. It does however eliminate the pagan gods from the picture altogether.

One of the motivations for this study is because the early chapters of Genesis have been used by those who do not believe in God to discredit the Bible and faith in God. The tactic is to prove that Genesis contradicts science and therefore the whole Bible is wrong and can be discarded. I hope to avoid adding fuel to the fire by not making claims that the Bible does not. I am not asking you give up any beliefs that you have, but to carefully consider them and to be careful not to read into the text what is not there. Watch out for assumptions, especially believing that our values, our understanding of the world, and our thought processes are the same as the people in Genesis, because they are not.

The conflict, both past and present, between science and theology is that neither is content to accept they are two different realms requiring different methods of inquiry. By definition science deals with the material nature, things that can be examined by the senses, tested, and measured. Theology deals with the realm that cannot be accessed by such things ("Now faith is the assurance of things hoped for, the conviction of things not seen" [RSV]). This does not mean that one cannot inform the other. Theology can give moral guidance to science and purpose (Ps. 8). Science can shed light on the handiwork of God (Ps. 19:1). Our culture has become so materialistic that everything is viewed from the material perspective. This causes people, even religious ones, to only view creation as if it were a material act but Genesis is telling us that it is something quite different; it is a spiritual act preparing the earth for us. There are many scientists who believe in God and that He was intimately involved bringing the universe into existence and continues to sustain it. This does not prevent their studying His handiwork and striving to understand the workings of the material.

8

Humans Become Dominant

THE NEXT THREE OR FOUR chapters will cover Genesis 2 and 3. There are a lot of opportunities to delve into various topics such as evolution and the fall; however, I want to stick pretty much to the text, again trying to understand it as the Israelites would have, and only bring in a few other points as needed. The other topics will be studied later. Chapter 4 is a peek at a dysfunctional family. Chapter 5 shows them fulfilling the charge they were given in 1:28 to be fruitful and fill the earth.

The bulk of Genesis 2 is often viewed as a recap of the seven days. In some sense this may be true, but it certainly is not just a recap for the following reasons. With the transition from chapter1 to chapter 2, Genesis leaves the creation of everything else and focuses on human beings. In verses 1:26–30 the creation of animals is given and of humans at the end of Day 6. What is expected of humans is delineated. Then chapter 2:1–3 says that God rested and made the seventh day special. There is not the usual evening and morning bracketing Day 7 as is in the other six. We review the break and change of emphasis mentioned before and indicated in 2:4 by the phrase "These are the generations of

. . ." This phrase or its equivalent is used several more times in the Bible (Gen. 2:4; 5:1; 6:9; 10:1; 11:10, 27; 25:12, 19; 36:1, 9; 37:2; Num. 3:1; Ruth 4:18; 1 Chron. 1:29. Except for Gen. 2:4, all are followed by a genealogy). Verses 2:4b–6 repeat the creating of plants, which was done in verses 1:9–13, except that here they seem to be cultivated plants. (What happened to Days 4, 5, and 6 if this is just a recounting)? Cultivated plants leads more naturally to the planting of the Garden of Eden. Man is mentioned (2:7) again because of his upcoming role in the story.

Word studies can quickly become boring but a little needs to be done here to avoid confusion that comes from the translation. First is a look at the Hebrew word adam. It is translated "man" (human would work just as well in most cases) over 500 times in the OT. In Genesis chapters 1–5, it used with the definite article 22 times (1:27; 2:7 (twice), 23, 25; 3:8, 8, 12, 20, 22, 24; 4:1); with attached preposition three times (2:20; 3:17, 21); with neither one nine times (1:26; 2:5; 4:25; 5:1 (twice), 2, 3, 4, 5). It is a Hebrew word and as such would not have been used by Adam and Eve. Hebrew was simply not spoken when they lived. Their names are, therefore, not historical names but are given by the Hebrew writer for some purpose. This is that these historical individuals represent something beyond themselves. The word adam is used generically and in the plural in verses 1:26; 2:5. See reference 14, chapter 6, for a more comprehensive analysis.

(There are other Hebrew words that are translated man in the OT. Ish carries the sense of man, husband, or individual and used over 700 times in the OT, but used only 4 times in Genesis 1–5 [2:23, 24; 4:1, 23]. Enosh and its plural anashim are used as man or mortal but not in chapters 1–5. Enash is used as man or mortal 19 times. Other words are used less often for a total of 14 different words.)

A word or two of caution about the following comments is needed. Everyone has ideas about what happens in chapters 2 and 3. These ideas are probably different and cover a whole range of possibilities. So you can take or leave what I am about to present. These are just ideas I have developed over many years, especially studying the conflict some people have between science and the Bible. Some of the ideas have probably come from many sources amalgamated together and I cannot tell you now of a source for most of them.

From the above discussion I am led to conclude that the creation of humans included more than a couple of individuals. However, those two individuals are very important to the biblical story and cannot be dismissed. They are real human beings who serve as archetypes for the human race. (Archetype: a representative of a group in whom all others in the group are embodied.) Further evidence that they were not alone comes from the story of Cain: he was able to find a wife, he was afraid of being harmed by other people, and he established a city (which requires many other people). Another point, which will be discussed later, comes from the NT. First Corinthians 15:42–50 discusses the difference between the physical and spiritual using Adam and Christ. It calls Adam the first and Christ the last. This cannot mean the physical because multitudes of physical beings have appeared after Christ. This will be taken up later.

Another point to consider here is about making man in God's image. What exactly does this mean? It obviously does not mean the physical body. They are to have dominion over the other creatures, probably as a representative of God. The Hebrew word for "make" used in 2:16 is asah and translated "appointed" in 1 Samuel 12:6 (". . . the Lord is witness, who appointed Moses and Aaron . . ." [RSV]). Moses and Aaron existed when they were appointed. Does this mean that in Genesis 1:26 when man is to be "made" that he already physically exists and the "making" is being appointed?

Except for the genealogy in 1 Chronicles, Adam and Eve are never mentioned again in the OT after the first five chapters of Genesis. This means they were not important as individuals to the Israelites. The Israelites only refer to individuals as far back as Abraham. Five short passages in the NT refer to Adam or both of them (the three passages in the next paragraph and genealogically in Luke 3:38, Jude 14). Eve is mentioned alone in 2 Corinthians 11:3.

The profile of Adam becomes complex. A larger statement is made than just the biography of an individual, since reference is made to him in the NT (Rom. 5:12–14; 1 Cor. 15:42–50; 1 Tim. 2:12–15). When adam is used generically it is talking about human beings as a species, when used with the definite article it is about an individual as a human representative, and when used alone it is as a proper name. Adam and Eve are certainly included in those humans that are created, simply not the only ones and not necessarily the first ones. They are selected as individuals for a specific task(s) as becomes the pattern through the rest of the Bible. Genesis 1 recounts the creation of humanity in God's image and that He has created an ordered space for them. That it is generic is indicated because of the indefinite article and plural term used. Genesis 1 does not report mechanisms or processes used in creation but that it is His work.

Just as chapter 1 begins with the non-ordered state of the cosmos and brings order to it, so chapter 2 begins with the non-ordered state of the terrestrial realm. Now humans are involved in bringing order and functioning in that space. A sacred space will be established on earth. This process will very much involve Adam and Eve.

Verse 2:7 needs further examination. A quick reading of the English seems to indicate that God simply scooped up a handful of dust and fashioned a man out of it as a potter would do, then breathed life into it. It is not necessarily that simple. The word translated as "formed" is used 42 times in the OT including nonmaterial ways. Therefore, "formed" need not mean a material act (Zech. 12:1 says, "The Lord, who stretches out the heavens, who lays the foundation of the earth, and who forms the spirit of man within him" [NIV]). Other passages in the same vein include 2 Kings 19:25; Psalms 33:15; 74:17; 94:20; 139:16; Isaiah 43:1, 21; 44:2, 21, 24; 45:11; 45:7, et al.

Dust from the ground does not contain the elements that make up humans (rich organic soil would not be dust). Soil is mainly silicon while the human body is (besides water) mainly carbon and not silicon. The phrase "dust to dust" from 3:19 is referring to mortality. After all, it was access to the tree of life that sustained Adam and Eve, not an inherent immortality. Death came into play after they were denied access. All of us are like Adam, formed from dust (Ps. 103:14) and have the breath of God (Is. 42:5). Animals also had the breath of life (Gen. 7:22). Thus the forming of Adam was not unique; all of us were formed by the same process (Job 10:9). This is discussed more fully in reference 14, chapter 8.

Verses 8–17 tell of the planting of the Garden of Eden and the placing of man there. Notice that names are not given for Adam and Eve until later in chapter 3, until then they are referred to as "the man" and "the woman." Rather than being formal names, these designations could be more of a title. Adam is "The Man" and Eve is "Life," becoming archetypes for all of humanity.

I had always thought that the garden was given as a paradise-like home for humans (in fact it is used this way all the time in current literature). This time a careful reading and a reconsidering indicates something else. The man was actually placed there to be the gardener and given work to do (2:15). As a reward for his efforts, the man was allowed the benefits of the garden except for the fruit of the tree of knowledge (2:16–17). Adam was alone when this restriction is given (2:17). Eve is created after the charge is given but she knew about it in 3:2. Did God tell her separately, did Adam tell, or did it come along as a part of the forming process?

God is described as walking in the garden in 3:8. Thus the garden is a sacred place on earth where God may meet with humans. His primary abode is in the heavens. This concept is carried out in the biblical story. To review, the building of the tower of Babel may have been less of a place for humans to ascend to heaven and more of a way for God to descend to earth. Perhaps that is why the pyramids in Egypt and elsewhere were built to allow the gods to come down and dwell with the deceased Pharaoh or ruler. Noah's emergence from the ark gave rise to another type (limited) of sacred space: that of the altar in Genesis 8:20 that is continued by the following patriarchs. In Exodus the tabernacle is constructed and becomes the place for the presence of God (Ex. 40:34–35). The same holds for the temple (1 Ki. 9:1–9). That would explain why the destruction of the temple was so devastating to the Israelites; they no longer had a place to meet with God. The importance of the temple to the Jews is really highlighted by the urgency to rebuild it after the return from Babylonian captivity. The books of Ezra and Nehemiah relate the return and the struggles to rebuild the temple and the walls of Jerusalem. The prophets Haggai and Zechariah had to continually urge the people to keep up the work. The role of the man in the garden becomes that of the contact between God and humans. One can trace the progression of a human intermediary through the Bible. Examples would include Adam, maybe Enoch, Noah, Abraham, Jacob, Moses, Aaron, and the high priests of the tabernacle and temple, culminating in Christ. Since Christ, the human intermediary is not needed on earth as we are the temple of God. Our bodies are now called the temple of God because He dwells in us (1 Cor. 3:16; 6:19). Even more we become the priesthood (1 Pet. 2:9).

I concluded from this that Genesis does not say Adam and Eve were necessarily the first physical humans nor does it imply that we all are direct descendants from them. However, we suffer the consequences of their sin. More about this when we study Genesis chapter 3.

9

Adam's Task

FIRST, A QUICK RECAP FROM the last chapter: at the creating of humans in Genesis 1:26–27, more than a couple of individuals were created. This conclusion comes strictly from the biblical text: (1) the plural form of the word is used and both male and female are mentioned, (2) the activities related to Cain after his sin in chapter 4 involved a lot of other people, and (3) the comparison of Adam to Christ in 1 Corinthians 15 shows Adam being the first only in respect to Christ being the last. This is spiritual in nature, not physical.

The physical creation of humans took place before 1:26. The making (it could also be translated "appointing") in verse 1:26 is the process by which they became the "image of God" and were given dominion over the earth (1:28–30). This would include all humans. In chapter 2, Adam is given a special task in caring for the Garden of Eden (and Eve later). That this task includes the mediator between God and humans is discussed in 1 Corinthians 15. It is in this role of mediator that Adam is the first and Christ is the last in human form; not the physical creation of each.

That Adam was a real human being and was important is shown by his inclusion in three of the four genealogies. Genesis chapter 5 gives a lineage from Adam to the sons of Noah. First Chronicles 1–9 gives extensive genealogies beginning with Adam. Matthew 1 gives a genealogy starting with Abraham and ending with Jesus. In Luke 3:23–38 the genealogy starts with Jesus and goes back to God. There is a difference between Matthew and Luke from David to Jesus. Matthew, who is Jewish, goes through Solomon while Luke, who is Gentile, goes through Nathan as sons of David. Matthew 1:16 acknowledges Joseph as the husband of Mary and Luke calls Jesus the "supposed" son of Joseph. None of these genealogies claim that Adam was the first human being. These are more about the legitimacy of the Jewish claim to the kingdom of God.

In Acts 17:22–31 Paul is trying to counteract the polytheism that still exists for the Athenians. He describes their unknown god as being the God whom he is proclaiming. This God created everything, is Lord of heaven and earth, and does not live in shrines made by humans. He is not served by humans but gives life to them. This is in stark contrast to the functioning of their gods. Not only that, but that He made all nations from one. In Acts 17:26, some versions of the Bible say, "He made from one man . . ." (NIV), while others say only "He made from one . . ." (RSV). There is no word for "man" in the Greek and is supplied by the translators. From the context, "from one nation . . ." would probably be a better translation (which is the promise made to Abraham in Gen. 17:4).

In conclusion, I see nothing in the Bible to support a claim that Adam and Eve were the first humans created and that we all descended from them (nor nothing to deny it). Those who support such a claim usually do so in support of some other doctrine (such as "original sin," to be covered later) or by atheists to discredit the Bible. This by no means diminishes the importance of Adam and Eve. Adam was the first human through whom people could interact with God; Christ was the last because we have now been granted access directly through him.

Because of all the baggage associated with people's hang up on material things, verse 1:27 is usually glossed over. ("So God created man in his own image, in the image of God he created him, male and female he created them" [Gen. 1:27 NIV]). Yet it is probably the most profound and is really the central point of the whole creation account. Genesis was not written to inform us of the details of how everything came to exist but is written to tell us who did it, what our relationship is to Him, and what our responsibility is. We were given the intellect to work on understanding the material. The story of Adam and Eve was not to describe our material beginning and continuity but to describe our relationship.

From John Walton (reference 14, pages 194–196, condensed): Although this may not be a comprehensive list of all that it means to be in God's image, we can identify several aspects. We have an assigned role with an inherent function. We are stewards to subdue and rule, which differentiates us from all other creatures. The image is our core identity and who we are, and is interwoven in our nature; not something that we take on for ourselves or develop. Being in His image transforms us into something spiritual in nature. We stand in as His substitute. We represent His presence in a sacred space. The world's view of God is us. We are His work in the truest possible sense. And finally, we have a family relationship; we are His people, His offspring (Acts 17:28).

For the first time in Genesis 2:18, something in creation is described as "not good"; that is, that the man should not be alone. So God says that He will make a helper. Verse 2:19 shows how we must be careful in trying to come up with a sequence of events. It would almost sound like there was a special creation of animals just for this event. But the animals have already been mentioned in Day 6. We are already past Day 7 and the resting, so something else is going on. The parading of the animals would not have been in the Garden of Eden. What about the naming and how does it relate to finding a helper? Who made the decision in verse 2:20 that none of the animals would be a suitable helper? God could have certainly known what the result would be, so the process was probably for Adam's benefit. The rejection of any of the animals as a suitable helper emphasizes the distinction between humans and the animals (e.g., that we are created in the image of God).

The woman is formed in chapter 2:21–24. The word for formed (fashioned) is the same as in Psalms 33:15 ("he who fashions them all . . ." [RSV]) and many other places. The woman is formed from a part of the man. This passage is only incidentally concerned with details or mechanisms. Its purpose is to show the relationship between man and woman, how it is carried out and their relationship to God. Too much emphasis has been placed on the mechanics of the process. The thrust of the passage is the relationship that is to exist between the Man and the Woman. Adam is not used as a proper name until 3:17; Eve in 3:20.

The Hebrew word translated as "rib" in English is used about 40 times in the OT. This is the only place in the OT where the word is translated rib; usually is a more substantial piece; hill, 2 Sam 16:13. All other times it is used architecturally as "side," like rooms along the side of a building (for example, Ex. chapters 25–38; 1 Kings chapters 6 and 7; Ezek. chapter 41). Thus more than just a single bone is probably involved; the man even says, "This at last is bone of my bones and flesh of my flesh . . ." (2:23 RSV). Early translations of the OT into other languages did not translate the word as "rib." It was not until the first English translations that it was translated as "rib" and the word has stuck.

The word translated as "deep sleep" is used seven times as a noun and seven times as a verb in the OT. "Trance" would perhaps be a better word (Gen. 15:12; Job 4:13; Dan. 8:18). The whole process could be a vision that the man had of himself where one of his sides is taken to form woman rather than something actually physical. I don't know how the Israelites at Sinai would have understood this. But the main point is that man and woman are intimately related in their forming and are intimately related in their lives. This defines and establishes marriage and certainly rules out same sex marriage. It is interesting that the man is the one who leaves his family to form a new one.

Sometimes, especially when reading English versions of the Bible, we tend to work with and assume the simplest interpretation of events that are based more on our own lives and experiences rather than look for a deeper meaning. It is easy to use the idea of a rib because it is easy to visualize. This misses the much more profound action that is taking place. By taking a side instead of just a rib there is a much greater connection between the two. Adam thinks Eve is more than just a rib in 2:23. It is likely that a whole side was used and Eve literally becomes a helper beside him. Thus marriage becomes a reuniting of those sides into an intimate relationship. They become helpers of each other "side by side." Although God could certainly do such radical surgery and healing, it is also possible that it was a vision Adam saw while he was in a trance. This would be very similar to the experience Jacob had in wrestling with the angel in Genesis 32:24–32 or the dream he had in Genesis 28:10–17. God uses this method to communicate His will. A detailed account of the above concepts is given in reference 14, pages 70 to 81 so I will not dwell on it here.

It is probably time to repeat my speech. This study is to try to understand the creation account and to do so, as much as possible, from the biblical text itself. But this means as the Israelites, to whom it is written, would have understood it in the original language, then we can apply it to ourselves. I want to show that the attacks against the Bible in particular and Christianity in general by claiming contradictions between current science and biblical belief are off base. Science deals with the physical and religion with the spiritual. They deal with two different realms with two different methods of inquiry that are mutually exclusive. Even when they converge to common points of interest, the questions are different and the methods are different.

10

The Fall
and Its Effect

THIS CHAPTER AND THE NEXT one will cover Genesis 3. In this chapter the basic events will be examined and the next chapter the consequences of those events. There will of necessity be some overlap. The Israelite perspective may be harder to achieve.

In chapter 3 the events of the fall are told; that is, how sin entered the world. The term fall is not used in the Bible and the events are not mentioned again until Paul refers to them in the NT. Careful reading is required to avoid assumptions. Adam is placed in the garden as a caretaker. God sees that Adam needs help and Eve is given to be the helper. There is no indication of how long Adam was alone. There is also no indication that Adam and Eve spent all their time in the garden and never left it until they were kicked out.

The appearance of the serpent at the beginning of chapter 3 is a bit of an enigma. He is not identified nor given any introduction; only his nature is given and the fact that he is a "wild creature that the Lord God had made." Eve, like Harry Potter, does not seem surprised that she can understand him. Remember that this was written to the Israelites, not to Adam and Eve. Serpents were very prominent in Egyptian motifs and would be very familiar. The most commonly known Egyptian serpent is the asp, a cobra variety (pethen in Hebrew, translated four times as asp and twice as viper). Most of the references in the OT are generic for serpent (in Hebrew, nachush), mentioned about 32 times. In Aaron's encounter with Pharaoh's sorcerers, the Hebrew word used is tannin. The few other places in the OT where it is used translate it as dragon or sea monster (Ps. 148:7). A few other places are specific: adder, asp, cockatrice, and viper. (All of the references are venomous varieties; probably why the translators used serpent instead of just snake.) Genesis gives no indication of the size, type, or appearance of the serpent.

No details are given about what led up to the encounter between Eve and the serpent so we will have to figure it out from other parts of the Bible. We cannot apply the NT perspective because that is not how the Israelites would have seen it. Because so little to do is made about it in the OT, the events must have not seemed too out of place to them or of much interest. The character of the serpent is not developed. This particular serpent is not equated to Satan. Nothing in the Bible suggests that the serpent in Genesis and the one in Revelation are the exact same creature. In fact there is more to suggest that they are not. Only in Revelation is Satan referred to as a serpent and there is no reason to assume that it is the same one. (Rev. 12: 9, "And that great dragon was thrown down, that ancient serpent, who is called the Devil and Satan, the deceiver of the whole world" [ASV]. Rev. 20:2 is similar.) It may only be an insulting epitaph. The adjective applied to the serpent is translated variously as subtle, wily, shred, prudent, or clever in the OT. It is not necessarily inherently evil or good. We are never told his intentions, but notice how devious and misleading he is.

An Israelite reader would not have identified the serpent with Satan, but recognize the deleterious effects of the temptation. The Israelite reader would not have thought of the serpent as being evil or bent on destruction of mankind, but would have thought of him as more of a disruptive agent. He would have understood the temptation and consequences much as we do and the serpent had a role in planting evil among humanity. Jumping ahead briefly, the "seed" of the serpent is the evil that results and continues as an ongoing struggle for humans.

As an aside, the character of Satan is not developed much in the OT in which he is known as an adversary, the hater, or the accuser, and appears in only four verses (1 Chron. 21:18; Ps. 109:6; Zech. 3:1–2) besides Job 1 and 2. Devils, referring to demons, is used only four times in the OT (Lev. 17:7; Deut. 32:17; 2 Chron. 11:15; Ps. 106:37).

It is very likely that the serpent was not in the garden but spoke to Eve outside it. Why would the serpent be allowed in? Were there any other animals in it? The naming of the animals by Adam in Genesis 2:18–20 was probably done outside the garden. There is nothing in the text one way or the other. Notice that the serpent never told Eve to eat the forbidden fruit; only that she would not really die and would become like God. The actual eating of the fruit was a decision made, first by Eve and then Adam, strictly on their own. That decision rested on two assumptions: that they would not really die and that they would be equal to God. The Devil didn't make them do it; they did it on their own.

In verse 3:6 there are three reasons given as to why Eve ate the fruit because (1) it was good for food, (2) it looked good, and (3) it would make her wise). (How it came to be associated with an apple, I have no idea. It must have been from some other piece of literature.) Much theology has been developed about these three reasons. Most of that theology is by trying to equate Eve's reasons to the vanity of the world in 1 John 2:16 (the lust of the flesh, the lust of the eyes, and the pride of life). There is nothing in the text that would indicated the Israelites would make that association. There is nothing that indicates that John was referring back to this verse. Instant death did not result when Eve and Adam ate the forbidden fruit, seeming at the moment to validate the serpent's assertion. Death would come because they no longer had access to the tree of life. Because no other humans can have access, we all suffer death because all have sinned (Rom. 5:12–14). First Corinthians 15:42–50 is about how we overcome this, or rather how Christ has overcome it for us.

Eve's action in eating of the forbidden fruit probably seemed like a small thing to her. After all, what could possibly go wrong by having a little taste? The lesson for us is that small actions can have severe consequences. We may do things that seem unimportant or trivial to us, but result in huge effects. This may be compared to an example from the Chaos theory called The Butterfly Effect. It was popularized in the book and movie Jurassic Park. It is stated something like "if a butterfly flaps its wings in South America, the disturbance in the atmosphere will escalate and cause a major blizzard six months later in the Alps."

That is an exaggeration, of course, but the Chaos theory does show that small changes in initial conditions or parameters of a process can result in widely varying results. The concept extends into other areas such as a small, offhanded remark has ruined many a friendship. We need to look beyond ourselves to see the effects of our actions. The idea of consequences is discussed more in the next chapter.

We will take a brief (and far from comprehensive) look at how God communicates. There are people today who claim that God talks directly to them. Adam and Eve are, of course, the first to whom God talked (Adam in 2:16), but we are not given any details about how the conservation took place. They detected the presence of God by hearing Him (3:8). His "walking" in the garden is probably a metaphor. Lots of God's actions in the Bible are described in terms of human anatomy; this does not mean that God looks exactly like us, rather He only uses familiar terms so that we can understand. It seems God talks directly to humans up to Abraham, after which it appears that less direct methods are used.

After this Eve succumbed to the temptation and ate of the fruit. She then gave some to Adam. As predicted, their eyes were opened. They immediately saw a problem and devised a solution to it. They quickly learned that you can run from God but you cannot hide. Why were they afraid? They were in the garden when God confronted them (the fruit was in the garden, after all). Adam blamed Eve for the sin (and by implication, God for giving her to him) and Eve blamed the serpent. God said they were all guilty and punished all three. The consequences of the sin have been discussed much ever since. I will go into that more in the next chapter. From the very start, Adam and Eve made a choice in the Garden of Eden that affected the world forever.

Throughout life we are confronted with situations in which a choice has to be made among two or more alternatives. These can range from minor day-to-day decisions to something that can have a major impact on our lives or the lives of many others. Each choice will have consequences. Sometimes the consequences are well thought out and anticipated. Others may be unexpected, yet have a profound effect. Our desires and emotions can influence a choice much more than logic or a full consideration of the consequences. After making a choice we must then be prepared to accept the responsibility for it and its consequences.

Too often choices are made without considering the effect on others. When the Bible speaks of "visiting the sins of the father" on future generations, it is not so much of a punishment as a recognition of how things work. Choices have to be made. But consideration should be given beyond the immediate impact. Many people's choices are affected by the past. They delve so deeply into the past that the future is sacrificed and the present is lost. The infatuation with the past can take many forms. For some it is a desire to return to the way things were or were perceived to be in the past. For others it can be regret for the past and a wish that things had been different. Either way can have undesired consequences. Even church leaders today can spend so much effort wanting to restore things as they were 50 to 100 hundred years ago that they lose the present generation and sacrifice the church of the future.

There are lingering questions that a sentient being will have even though they may not recognize the fact. The first question is, "Who am I?" The problem with the approach taken to try to answer the question was the assumption that the answer existed and one had only to find it. The actual answer is something one creates. Too often there is the tendency to let it be defined by others or by circumstances. Every person has the opportunity to choose who they are. It is not something that is handed to them but requires thought and work in order to achieve. It usually involves answering the question, "Who do I want to be?"

The second question asked after the first is answered is, "What do you want?" For some the answer may be only for the next moment, the next day, or some other short time period. Those who ponder the question more deeply will consider it in terms of their entire life. Some may answer, "I just want to be happy" with no more definition. Try to figure that one out. Happiness is more a result than a goal to be pursued. The same thought and hard work has to be done to choose what one wants before trying to achieve it. The trivial wants that many think about turn out to be satisfying for only a very short time. Such wants can be the newest video game, new clothes, a new car, or some other material possession. Even more abstract wants such as health, happiness, love, and such like can be elusive if not part of true life desires.

If you know who you are and what you want, then you need to answer, "Where am I going?" So many lives are lived without a direction or beacon to guide them. This is a choice that may be made at any stage in life. It takes a degree of maturity to make. Like the other choices, it may be revised throughout life. However, the consequences will not go away nor will the responsibility for those choices. To get where you want to go involves serious planning and evaluation of progress. Where you are going is a process and journey rather than trying to reach a final destination. It is easy to let someone else choose where you are going, which only lasts until they achieve their goals. For some it takes a dramatic event for them to choose where they are going. One does not always make the right choice, but consequences still result and one has to take responsibility. Too many people live their lives as if it were a game to finish first.

After the other questions are answered, we must then ask, "Why am I here?" Some have taken the approach that it is all predetermined and all you have to do is discover it (such as Rick Warren's book, The Purpose Driven Life). The truth is that you can choose why you are here. For some it is to enjoy the next moment, to achieve the next high. Some have chosen a life dedicated to helping others. Some have chosen to accumulate as much wealth as possible. All through history there have been those who use and exploit others. They have had the arrogant assumption that others are here only for the other person, without any idea why they might be here themselves. We hear stories often about ordinary people doing extraordinary things because they happened to be at the right place at the right time and made the choice to act. This effect is true even for seemingly small, unimportant events that yet have on impact on someone.

It is important for all of us to realize that we will be continually confronted with choices. The consequences are not always easy to see and evaluate, but it must be understood that they will appear. Acceptance of the responsibility is often hard to do and the tendency is to blame someone else. Notice in the daily news and in everyday lives how there are no wrongdoers, only victims.

11

Consequences

First a quick review. The serpent beguiles Eve concerning the forbidden fruit by telling her that she will not really die and it will make her wise. She succumbs and eats, then offers Adam some. She probably thought, as a good wife, that she should let Adam share in the benefits. Adam, as a good husband, follows her suggestion. There is probably a really good lesson here about how we can think we are helping someone when, in reality, we are causing them harm. But I am not wise enough to develop it. After eating, Adam and Eve are caught by God. After being caught they do what people always like to do when caught red handed: they played the blame game. Adam points to Eve as the cause and reminds God that, after all, you gave her to me. Eve in turn points to the serpent.

God pointed out that all three were guilty and there was enough blame to go around. There is also enough punishment to go around. I think it is interesting that the punishment is meted out in the order in which each sinned (3:14–19). The serpent is to be cursed above all other creatures (I still don't like snakes). Crawling on his belly and eating dust are likely metaphors, and his diet does not really become dirt. This is probably more like when one racer brags to his opponent, "You'll eat my dust." The serpent did not have legs that are now taken away. His attack position is with the front third of his body raised and the rest flat on the ground. He will not be able to move in this position; he will have to go flat to move, which makes him more vulnerable.

There is to be enmity between the seed of the serpent and the seed of the woman. Some see this as a description of the battle between Christ and the Devil. Although it may be a very good analogy, there is nothing in the Bible that brings this out. If it were true, I would have expected it to be discussed in Romans 5 or 1 Corinthians 15. Try to understand Genesis 3:15 as the Israelites would have understood it. The important seed of the serpent is not so much his offspring, as it is bringing sin and evil into the world. There is no prediction of who the victor will be in the battle between the two seeds; instead it indicates there will be an ongoing struggle between them. Each will give potentially mortal blows to the other. Soon after the prediction of the seed of the woman bruising the head of the serpent and the serpent striking his heel, the women's shoe with a spike high heel was invented. And maybe the heavy clog heel.

Some might consider the punishment meted out to the woman to be the greatest. I am not experienced in the pain of childbearing so cannot say much about it. The husband who has rule over her is referred to in 1 Timothy 2:12–15. This has been discussed for countless eons and will continue to be. Adam's punishment is that making a living got a lot harder. In the end, death will really come to all and their mortal bodies will decay. Eve is officially given her name in 3:20. Describing her as "the mother of all living" does not mean that we are all direct descendants of her. Animals are a part of all living, too. The phrase is used in the same sense as "the father of all" as used in 4:20–22.

The problem now is that people know good and evil just as God does (3:22). (Notice that God describes Himself in the plural.) The forbidden tree was described as the tree of the knowledge of good and evil, not knowledge in general. If people are allowed to eat of the tree of life, they can live forever, so they are denied access to it. This is the way the punishment of death is carried out, not something immediate. Man is ejected from the Garden of Eden. Verse 23 says God sent man forth while verse 24 adds that God drove man out. To limit access, a cherubim and a flaming sword are put in place to guard it. I had always read this as being at the entrance of the Garden of Eden, but what it really says is "the way to the tree of life." The death result was not immediate but was caused by being cut off from the tree of life in Genesis 3:22. This consequence thus propagated to all humans thereafter.

We usually assume that the sin was disobedience; however, it was more likely the reason for the disobedience. The more serious sin was that they wanted to become like God, according to Genesis 3:6. In today's world the idea of sin has lost its significance. It is usually equated to a crime that is far more restricted than the biblical view. It is often considered as a "burden to be borne" or a "debt to be repaid." These are more the consequences of sin but do point the way to its resolution. It appears often in the OT to mean "missing the mark" or failing to meet an objective (Prov. 8:36; Is. 65:20). It appears in various disguises such as rebellion, transgression, iniquity, and guilt.

A more important approach to understanding sin is to think about what it does rather than what it is. Sin is a threat to our relationship to God, which results in alienation. The example here is the banishment of Adam from the Garden of Eden. A relationship with God was His intention in the creation of human beings (which is why we were created in His image). Sin disrupts this relationship that is human's deepest desire. The stages of the reestablishment of what was lost in Genesis 3 is documented in the rest of Scripture. The previous ideas of sin are not mutually exclusive. The OT does not speak of Adam bringing sin on everyone, even though the effects are seen throughout.

The fall was from the decision to be like God, as seen by the serpent's words (3:5), the woman's response (3:6), God's assessment (3:22), and the reason for banishment (3:22). The way in which the man and the woman became knowledgeable was only in respect to what the tree had to offer; knowledge of good and evil, not that they became omniscient or omnipotent. They were trying to place themselves at the center of things. But the fear of the Lord is the beginning of wisdom and He is the source of it. His presence establishes a center of wisdom. It concerns seeking order in all categories of life. Wisdom is the result when we promote it, procure it, and practice it. Its source is not in oneself specifically or humankind in general.

By eating the fruit, Adam and Eve were trying to make themselves a center of wisdom. It is very much a childish response, such as "I can do it myself" or "I want to do it my way." These are not necessarily a rejection of authority as much as an insistence on independence. It is a way of asserting, "It's all about me." This has characterized humanity ever since. True wisdom is acquired through a process (as Yoda tried to teach Luke Skywalker in The Empire Strikes Back). It would seem from 1:28 that God did not intend to withhold wisdom from humanity. What Adam and Eve tried to do was short circuit the process, speed it up, and obtain it illegitimately due to a lack of patience. The import of their sin was about the wisdom that was taken. Thus the fall was not just an ordinary test case where the tree provided for an opportunity for obedience or disobedience. It was far more because the tree had inherent properties. Still we all suffer the consequences of the fall.

Because the OT never again refers to Adam and Eve or the fall, we must look to the NT for its significance to us. This involves looking at the three passages (four if you want to include the use of Eve as an example in 2 Cor. 11:3) where Paul refers to the events. In all three he assumes the addressees are familiar with the story. What makes this interesting is that Paul considered himself as an apostle to the Gentiles. This came as a result of opposition from the Jews at Antioch Pisidia (Acts 13:46) on his first missionary journey. He still went first into the synagogue at each place he visited (like Acts 14:1). The church at Rome was believed to be predominantly Gentile although there seemed to be a lot of Jews as well (Rom. 4:1). Corinth was a Roman city, so most of the Christians were probably Gentile. Timothy had a Gentile father and a Jewish mother, thus Timothy was probably well versed in the OT. He was in Ephesus, a Gentile church, when Paul wrote to him.

The debate over human origins and the mechanism of creation obscures the real message of Genesis. We need the help of the three NT passage to regain the sense of what it is all about. There is a tendency to take the egocentric view that everything is about me and my salvation. This narrow view dulls the vision of the broader view. This is really about the kingdom of God. After God created humans in His image in verse 1:27, their purpose, their job, their vocation is given in verse 1:28. They are to complete the task of creation by being God's representatives to subdue the world and rule over it. To accomplish the task, two humans are plucked from the others and given a special work. They are placed in the Garden of Eden, which is God's sacred space where humans may have contact with God. (This is the same function as assigned to the most holy place [the holy of holies] first in the tabernacle and then in the temple in which only the high priest is allowed once a year.) From there they are to complete bringing order into the world. By their sin Adam and Eve have broken this connection. As the ones in the garden, they were the only ones who had access to the tree of life. Now that they are no longer there, death will come to all.

Until the tabernacle is built, the connection to God remains broken. Up until then, there is no written law that we know of; we only know that Genesis was written at that time to the Israelites to prepare them for what was to be expected of them. After Adam and Eve failed at the task, it is not clear if any others took up the slack. It could be that Noah did. It certainly was passed on to Abraham, and thus to the nation of Israel. They are to understand that is why they are promised a land. In a sense it is to become their equivalent of Eden. It is described in glowing terms. The nation of Israel is to be the solution to the problem caused by the disobedience of Adam. As it turns out, the solution becomes part of the problem. They continue to disobey God. Thus Paul says in Romans 5:14 that death reigned from Adam to Moses. Adam's sin is not only against humanity but against all of creation. The glory and honor of Psalms 8:5 has been tarnished. God's project for all of creation has been put on hold because of the failing of humans. As a successor to the work that Adam blotched, Abraham is called in Genesis 17:1–4 to take up the task of completing creation. Thus the nation of Israel is formed as a vehicle for subduing and ruling the earth. Israel itself does no better job than its predecessors. The remedy finally appears in the form of Christ. This is the gist of the discussion in 1 Corinthians 15:12–49. Adam's and Christ's natures and roles are contrasted in 15:44b–49. Whereas our focus has been on ourselves and our salvation, Paul says the focus is preserving the kingdom of God and getting the process of creation back on track and completed. This gives us the sense in which Adam was the first and Christ the last. It has nothing to do with material creation or origins.

"All have sinned and fall short of the glory of God" (Rom. 3:23 RSV). That this affects all of creation is expressed in Romans 8:22. The remedy has been provided and is available to all but not all have taken advantage of it. As an alienated people, we are now reconciled through Christ. He has overcome death, the last enemy, but the first one Adam introduced. When I first looked to Romans, I thought it would help me understand Genesis but as I got into it I learned that Genesis helped to understand Romans. Romans 1:24–32 sounds like it could be tomorrow's news headline. The sin we inherit from Adam is not through any biological connection, but through our human nature to disobey and want things our way. There is nothing in the text, OT or NT, that suggests that at birth or before there is sin residing in us. Sin is a result of our choices and our attitudes. As we deal with people today we find they feel no need of being saved because they have not sinned; therefore, we have nothing to offer that they need. This attitude has been pervasive for a long time and has been addressed many times. One instance is from 1973 in a book written by a noted psychiatrist, Karl Menninger, entitled What Ever Became of Sin?

12

Evolution

INEVITABLY IN ANY DISCUSSION OF Genesis, the subject of biological evolution comes up. The debate has ranged far and wide over the last 160 years or so and shows no sign of letting up. It is beyond the scope of this book to give a comprehensive critique of the controversy. This chapter is only to point to an approach to studying it. There are many resources available. The three books listed in the references at the end of this paragraph are recent works that give slightly different perspectives from ones who are both biologists and Christians: notable mainly because I have recently read them. You might want to look up the authors on Wikipedia before reading the books. All three authors are strong Darwinians, are prominent in biological circles and oppose both creationism and neo-atheists, and therefore have been attacked from both sides. Miller and Ruse try to deal with the doctrine of original sin. I am not competent to comment on biology issues but I do think they are a little weak on physics at times and how they interpret the early chapters of Genesis. I don't like arguments that include "it must have" or similar phrases. The philosophies, conclusions, and implications that the authors draw out must be recognized as opinions. Sometimes they are hard to separate. Realize this applies to any book you read. (Kenneth R. Miller, Finding Darwin's God; Michael Ruse, Can a Darwinian Be a Christian?; Francis S. Collins, The Language of God.) Read with caution.

The word evolution can cover a wide spectrum of ideas. Basically it means merely changing over time. Most often people mean that proposed by Charles Darwin in his 1859 book on origin of species (meaning biological species) now often called Darwinism. It is used by atheists for an attack on the validity of the Bible. It is the working mantra of most biologists today; all living things are descended from a single life form created by chance that through mutations produced all living species. One problem I have with that is if the conditions were right for it to happen once, why only once and why at only one particular time and place? The basic mechanism was that only those most fit to survive were able to reproduce. This is popularly known as "survival of the fittest." Biologists use the euphemism "natural selection." Such a process would require a considerable amount of time and a very old earth. A more rapid example given is how bacteria become drug resistant. The original evidence presented for this was the fossil record and comparative morphology. Currently presented evidence is in the genetic code. There are some problems in the history of the evolutionary process that I have not seen any solutions that are satisfactory to me, such as bi-sexual reproduction. Some time there would have had to be two individuals who survived the selection process but of different sexes. Biologists have theories but they too often involve "it must have" expressions, which don't satisfy me.

Five terms we hear a lot about today are genes, chromosomes, genomes, DNA, and RNA. DNA (deoxyribonucleic acid) is the hereditary material in almost all organisms. Nearly every cell in a person's body has the same DNA located in the cell nucleus. A small amount is found in the mitochondria that convert food into a form cell can use. The information in the DNA is stored as a code made up of four chemical bases abbreviated as A, G, C, and T. Human DNA consists of about 3 billion bases that are the same in all people for over 99% of them. The ones that are different can be used to identify the particular individual from whom they came. This has become a very powerful forensic tool as glorified in movies, TV, and novels. The sequence of the bases carries the information for building an organism. The bases form pairs of A with T and C with G that attach to a sugar molecule and a phosphate molecule. They form a ladder-like structure into two long spirals, known as the famous double helix. DNA can replicate itself, and certain functional sections of the DNA form genes. RNA is a messenger.

The entire set of chromosomes made up of the 3 billion base pairs of Human DNA is called the human genome. A huge worldwide project was initiated to map the entire sequence. A funding source, as with any huge project, was governments. The idea was to share data as it became available and coordinate the work. Some private work was instigated to take advantage of project for the purpose of patenting it and making money from it. A big conflict naturally arose that greatly hindered the project. The project was declared completed in 2003.

Genes, the hereditary unit we hear the most about, are the physical and functional units. Some, but not all genes, code for the makeup of the protein molecules. Human genes vary in size from a few hundred DNA bases to more than 2 million. It is estimated that humans have between 20,000 and 25,000 genes. Every person has two copies of each gene, one from each parent. Only a small percent (less than 1%) are slightly different in all people. The differences contribute to each person's unique physical features. Genes that have been identified with specific functions are given names. The package for the DNA in the nucleus of each cell is a chromosome and the set of chromosomes make up the genome. The genome is tightly coiled around proteins to support its structure and would be over six feet long if unwound. DNA structures are so small as to not be visible, even by a microscope, except during cell division. Humans have 23 pairs of chromosomes, 22 of which look the same and are identified by number, with number 1 being the largest with 2,000 to 2,100 genes and number 22 having 500 to 600 genes. Pair number 23 is called the sex chromosomes and are two different types called X and Y. Females have two X chromosomes and males have an X and a Y. Because every cell in the body has all 46 chromosomes, so-called sex-change surgeries are superficial only since each cell still has its original X and Y chromosome makeup.

All living organisms have parts of DNA sequences that are the same. There are regions in the DNA that seem to have no apparent function. These are often referred to as junk DNA. They are used by some researchers to link different species and construct an evolutionary path. Although they claim this is conclusive evidence that evolution took place, I would say, "Not so fast." Many times in science, especially in biology, things have been believed to have no function but later one is found. For example, it used to be said that people used very little of the brain's capacity. However, now it is thought that a large part of the brain is used with our vision and in identifying objects. Not only is the brain used in just the transmitting of the nerve impulses from the eye to the relevant section of the brain but also is used in processing the information and establishing connections.

Some biologists question whether natural selection would be sufficient although most believe so. There is also the question of how the first organism was formed and how it became "living." There is the idea of "irreducible complexity" that says a minimum number of organic elements must be present to have a living organism. The probability of it happening by chance is prohibitively low. There is a huge range among believers that any evolution happened, from outright denial to full acceptance. Take your pick. Was Jacob's deal with Laban in Gen. 30:31–43 a biblical example of evolution at work? We know that God was involved but it doesn't say so. Genesis says that there was a progression in the creation of life from simple to the more complex, and science says the same although the details are different.

Some evolutionists claim that all life originated from a single living organism in the oceans. The process had to be very complex with a lot of coincidences occurring. The process is far too involved to repeat here. It can be found in the references. Some have also proposed that all humans descended from a single pair of organisms of a pre-homo sapiens form.

Another proof cited for evolution comes from paleontology and anthropology. Fossils have been found in many, many places although they are formed only under certain conditions. The majority of them are not the actual thing itself but are formed in a process similar to what produces petrified wood. The organic specimen is buried in some sediment then the organic material decays and is replaced with mineral deposits. Under pressure and time the minerals harden into a replica of the organism. The process works best for aquatic organisms. Some more durable parts like bones and shells may be preserved. A few fossil sites are unique in providing an environment for preserving bones. Perhaps the most famous of these is the La Brea Tar Pits in Los Angeles where petroleum deposits are close enough to the surface for some to seep into depressions in the ground. The process happened like this: rain water formed a pond on top of the tar, and animals wandered in, assuming it was a pond of water. Soon, they became trapped in the tar, sank, and perished. It should not be expected that every past organism is represented by a fossil. Studies of the fossil record show a steady progression from simple life forms to more complex ones. The age of the fossil comes by determining the age of the matrix in which it was found. Afterward, fossils of the same type are assumed to be from the same period, regardless of where they were found.

A big part of anthropology that makes headlines in the media is the search for the evolution of humans. Several species of humanoids have been found, and it is usually not explained that the quantity of finds are limited. Often only a few bones are found and the researcher extrapolates them into a complete creature. Complete skeletons are a rare find. One of the goals of a paleontologist is to find fossils of the earliest humans. This is a quest that has been filled with much competition, controversy, and bitterness. Funding has been a continual problem for those involved. Probably because there is little perceived commercial benefit, funding sources are very fickle. Mostly they are foundations, philanthropists, institutions, and the like. The funding sources favor sponsoring the researchers with the highest perceived chance of success. Thus researchers are forced to choose their sites carefully and to try to come up with significant results as quickly as possible. There may be a pressure to announce results prematurely, exaggerate, or in rare, extreme cases, even falsify. (The most famous case was the Piltdown Man hoax.)

As a typical example and perhaps the most well-known of these anthropologists was Louis Leakey. He was able to receive grants from The National Geographic Society in the early 1960s and publish results in their magazine. This gave him widespread exposure. He was born to English missionaries in Kenya, the region he knew and worked in most of his life. There is a place called the Olduval Gorge that was rich in fossils. Leakey and his family and colleagues excavated there extensively, found a few bones, including skulls and a tooth, reconstructed them, and claimed they were from early humans.

Another find that received much attention was made in Ethiopia in 1974. It was a partial skeleton of a female. It is considered one of the most complete, even though it was only about 40% complete and consisted of hundreds of bones and bone chips. Geologists date the rock formation at 3.16 million years ago. The hip and knee joints of the leg that was found were like human joints, but no other bones resembled a human's. The skull was missing, but the fragments concluded the brain was small. A complete reconstruction was made of what the specimen would have looked like. Unfortunately many people believed that that the reconstruction was what was actually found. An exhibit toured the world amid much hype. This was the only skeleton found at this site. It was given the name Lucy (to make it seem more like an actual human) and proclaimed to be an early humanoid. This is an example of the nature of the race between paleontologists.

From this work the assertion is made that humans originated in East Africa and spread from there. Naturally that is where the fossils would be found because that is where the paleontologists were looking. The work is so difficult and so weakly funded that there are vast areas of the world not similarly searched. Because the number of artifacts is small, double checking and other forms of verification are not possible. The core of establishing scientific facts is verification through experiments, duplication of results, and thorough testing. Fields that study past events are not able to operate that way and have to rely on other methods such as similar finds, thus it is prudent to be very tentative and cautious about accepting conclusions from such work. This comment is not meant to deny that some researchers do excellent and significant work.

Next, I will talk about extinctions and fossil records. From the fossil record, the development of life was not a steady progression. Some estimates are that 90 to 99.9% of all species that ever existed are now extinct. There have been identified five dramatic mass extinctions in which a least 50% of the species went extinct in a very short (geologically speaking) time. The causes are not well understood but are most likely due to some sort of climate change caused by solar system events that affected the food chain. In population dynamics it is known that certain species wipe out other species. Of course the case of humans is the most observable because humans are the most efficient predators and the most documented, but they are not the only ones. The population of prey versus predator fluctuates routinely. It is believed that had not some other event wiped out the dinosaurs, the dinosaurs would have eliminated mammals. In the natural run of things, some species are going to become extinct. Ice ages, discussed later, were also a big factor.

The climate of the earth has been in a constant process of change and will continue to be. The latest extinction was 65 million years ago that wiped out the dinosaurs. Many causes have been suggested over the years with the latest being an asteroid impact that sent dust into the air that blocked the sun and caused the earth to become cold. Why the dinosaurs were so hard hit is not clear except that reptiles are cold blooded organisms. What happened to other reptiles? These events happened before the events described in the days of creation that tell of assigning functions to the created material of Genesis 1:1–2; hence, there would have been no human observers, no record of them, and in contrast to the extinction at the time of Noah, there is no need to mention them. Lots of actual bones of larger creatures have been found. Fossils of the same type are assumed to be from the same time period regardless of where they are found.

With regard to population explosion, although the earth is thought to have been formed 5 billion years ago at the same time as the entire solar system, life could not exist until the earth was capable of supporting it. The preparation would be much like that in Genesis 1:3–9a. The population of life has been sporadic, punctuated by the extinctions. Estimated by geologists to have occurred about 540 million years ago, the first real flourish of life is called the Cambrian Explosion. Other similar increases have been noted but less dramatic. Since the last extinction, the population of animals has increased at a geometric rate. The worry is that at some point the population of animals will exceed the ability of the planet to support them. The planet will survive but we may not.

Some evolutionists have proposed that evolution has reached its end and humans represent the ultimate result (and Genesis agrees with that assessment). There are many reasons that such conclusions have been reached, but foremost among these reasons is that humans interfere with the process in a number of ways, affecting the environment, controlled breeding, eliminating mutations, using up resources, and controlling selection. Biologists (and other scientists) claim that no other organism has had anywhere the same impact. Other scientists think that microorganism will ultimately be the surviving life form and cite the rapidity with which microorganisms adapt to become drug resistant and the struggle to produce new medicines. There is also the concern that the control of genetic research and/or biological weapons will not be sufficient to prevent disasters. The danger could be natural like Ebola or artificially produced through genetic research, whether accidental or intentional. The biosphere is far too complex to be understood or controlled, and what is desirable for one species may be detrimental to another. Malaria is a textbook example and is a mosquito-borne disease caused by a parasite, not a microorganism. People with malaria usually experience fever, chills, and flu-like illness. It is not treatable like bacteria; once in a person's system it is difficult to eliminate. It is estimated that in 2017 there were 219 million cases worldwide and 435,000 deaths. The poor tropical countries suffer the most. In the 1960s the mosquito carrier was almost eliminated by the use of the insecticide, DDT. The number of malaria cases decreased dramatically. DDT was found to be responsible for the deaths of large numbers of birds that ate the mosquitoes. Consequently, there was a worldwide ban on DDT. No substitute has been found that is as effective, allowing the mosquito populations to recover and the malaria cases to increase, thus protecting one group of species (birds) and causing an increase of misery and death in another (humans). Many people believe that vaccines cause autism in children and do not get their children vaccinated. Now some childhood diseases that had been almost eliminated are resurging.

13

Dating

BIBLICAL SCHOLARS SINCE NEW TESTAMENT times have been interested in the chronology of the Bible and the dates of various events. This may have been driven by a desire to predict when judgment day will occur. There was a flurry of activity in the seventeenth century. The most well-known of these was formulated by James Ussher, the Archbishop of Armagh and Primate of All Ireland, who published Annals of the Old Testament in 1650 (original was published in Latin with a long title). Others who formulated chronologies around the same period were John Lightfoot, Jose ben Halafta, Bede, Scalinger, Johannes Kepler, and Isaac Newton. All of them had the earth around 6,000 years old and even gave a date for its creation, sometimes down to the hour. They used the Julian calendar. Ussher's chronology eventually was incorporated in editions of the KJV Bible. People began to place Ussher's date on an equality with the text.

The method used by Ussher for determining the chronology was not limited to information in the genealogies as is generally believed although he did use them. He was influenced by the accounts in the apocryphal Book of Jasher. The date of 4000 BC for the creation of Adam came from the widely held belief at time of the age of earth as approximately 5600 years. They used 2 Peter 3:8—which says, "One day is with the Lord as a thousand years and a thousand years as one day"—to correspond with the six days of creation. Two thousand years from Adam to Abraham, 2,000 years from Abraham to Christ, and 1,600 years from Christ to Ussher. Christ would return in the year 2000 AD.

From the genealogies in Genesis 6 and 11, a chronology from Adam to Abraham can be created; however, tying it to world events is difficult and interpreting the ages and successions is not as easy as it might seem. From Abraham to Solomon is perhaps the most reliable data. From Solomon's temple to the Babylonian captivity is harder, mainly because of correlating the reigns of the kings of Israel and Judah. Ussher also used accounts from Babylonian, Greek, and Roman sources. He only brings it up to the Maccabean period. Using these methods give an uncertainty as to the year of Jesus's birth. Herod the Great's death was in 4 BC according to Josephus. Because Jesus was born before his death, Jesus would have to be born before 5 BC. Such considerations show that trying to establish ancient dates is fraught with difficulties and uncertainties. Needless to say, Ussher's chronology has fallen out of favor, yet some still stick to it. As I showed in earlier chapters, even if one accepts that the time from Adam to now is on the order of 6,000 years, the total time for all the acts of creation could be much, much longer.

Unless and until better data is found, I can work with the ages estimated by geologists, paleontologists, archeologists, or cosmologists. I can also accept things such as the fossil record, ice ages, mass extinctions, continual climate change, tectonic plates, limited evolution (but not evolution and evolutionists!), Big Bang, relativity, expansion of the universe, black holes, and astronomical distances and times. I also know that true science is an ever-changing field and so that to try to tie religion and science together is not only a mistake but also bad theology. They are two separate fields dealing with two separate realms. That does not mean that one cannot inform the other. In discussing some of the history of the earth, I will use ages estimated by the appropriate scientific community. You can take them or leave them but they help to establish a framework for talking about some phenomena. The ages are constantly being revised and there is not always consensus.

When we talk about the age of universe, we might wonder what then should be our position in respect to the age of the universe? Mine is that we should not try to establish any specific time before Abraham in Genesis chapter 12. The Israelites to whom Genesis was written would have had no interest in the topic and would add nothing to the primary message of the book; the one God of Israel is the one who made everything, is the one who is in control, and is the one to be worshipped. The pagan gods are false, are idols, and should be ignored. In talking about the earth and its history, I can accept the dates scientists give us until better information comes along. The sciences that study the history of the earth (geology, paleontology, archeology, cosmology, anthropology) are deductive sciences; that is, that they take existing data and try to reconstruct the events leading up to it. There is no experiment that can be devised to test most of the theories. Evidence can be used to support the theories or possibly falsify them. That is why they will remain theories. A wide variety of methods are used to estimate ages, and in general, the further back the date, the less accurate and precise the age. The possibility of error depends on the particular method. True scientists will admit the imprecision and chance of errors.

Geology, as presently understood, shows a very violent and turbulent history of the earth. It places an age of 4.5 billion years (I will use geological ages for this discussion.) Astrophysics would make this hard to pin down because the earth had formed gradually from an accumulation of interstellar dust coalesced over millions of years. What atmosphere existed was very toxic, and life did not appear until about a couple of billion years ago. There was a rapid increase in the number of species appearing 550 million years ago during what is known as the Cambrian Explosion that was mentioned earlier. Geology breaks time into eons, eras, and periods based mainly on life forms and geographical features. One method of establishing dates is by studying naturally occurring radioactive elements. They change into other elements by radioactive decay (emission of particles or energy). The rate is indeterminate for an individual atom, but the average is statistically constant for a large number. The time required for half of the atoms of a particular element to decay is called the half-life. Comparison of the quantity present with what was originally present can be used to determine the age of undisturbed rocks.

Ages of various features of the earth are determined by other means. For example, the age of the Grand Canyon is estimated by determining the current rate of erosion by silt flows, then by calculating the volume of soil extracted from the canyon and dividing it by the silt removal rate, the age can be estimated. This is an estimate because it assumes what the earlier flow rates have been and how hard the different layers of rock are, and no major disturbances such as earthquakes or volcanoes. Then estimates of the ages of the many layers of different rocks and soils can be made. Similar rocks found at other places that appear to be formed the same way are assumed to be the same age. Naturally there are limits to the accuracy but the results are good enough for lots of purposes. Like all geological ages, they are subject to revisions.

The age of the total universe itself has been revised many times and will probably continue to be. For a lot of work that cosmologist do a factor of two is good enough, but, of course, they would like it as accurate as possible. They use several different methods based on what is observable and what can be deduced from it. One method is estimating the distance to most distant galaxies, how fast they are moving, and from these data then estimating the time back to the point of the Big Bang.

Carbon-14 dating (^{14}C) is the most used and the most accurate dating method; therefore an explanation of carbon-14 dating can be found in a myriad of sources. Of the three isotopes of carbon, ^{14}C is the only one that is radioactive. It has a half-life of about 5,730 years, decays to nitrogen, and is constantly replenished. As cosmic radiation strikes the upper atmosphere, the radiation converts a small portion of the nitrogen back into ^{14}C. It is estimated that the atmosphere contains about 40×10^{12} metric tons of carbon; of that, about 60 tons are ^{14}C. Plants assimilate carbon from the atmosphere in the form of CO_2 through photosynthesis and release oxygen. (That is why green plants are so important to our survival.) The process ends when the plant dies. By comparing the radioactivity of a similar living plant with that of a dead one, the age of the specimen can be determined. Of course, this method is subject errors but has proven to be most accurate back to about 40,000 years.

14

Other Topics Related to Origins and Creation

IN THIS CHAPTER I WILL discuss some topics that are often raised when talking about creation and origins but have no direct connection to Genesis.

With regard to prehistoric life, the question is often raised as to where the dinosaurs and similar prehistoric creatures fit into the Genesis account. The answer is that they don't. The discovery of such fossils has only been in the last 200 years or so. The true nature of ones found before that time was unknown. At the time Genesis was written the people had no knowledge of prehistoric life forms so there would be no reason to mention them. The paleontological evidence shows that the extinction of the dinosaurs occurred long before humans were created. The sequence of the development of life from geology and paleontology parallels that from Genesis 1. That is that the simplest were formed first and each step of creation produced more complex organisms. It might be claimed that there is an important difference about whether sea organisms or plants came first. Genesis might make it appear that plants were first, but the details are just not that specific. The question could also be raised that if the first organisms were from the animal kingdom, what did they feed on? The bottom of the food chain is almost always from the vegetable kingdom. There is absolutely no conflict between Genesis 1 and the paleontology record because there is no overlap in the time covered by each.

As we continue, another topic often discussed around creation that has no connection to Genesis is the subject of ice ages. The topic is covered in almost any geology book; reference 2 is a very interesting account of effects of the last ice age. Ice ages have been pretty well confirmed as a feature of the history of the earth. The term is imprecise and can refer to long, cool periods or very cold ones. The ones of the highest rank are called glacial ages and the next lower rank as glaciations. They have varied greatly as to duration, intensity, and location. Inside each period there are many smaller variations. A quick summary of what is known or surmised in the last billion years: there have been two complete glacial ages and we are in the beginning of the third. The typical duration is 8 million years. The first one began about 800 to 900 million years ago and the second 200 to 300 million years ago. The third is just starting. During the time when a glacial age was not in progress, the climate was comparatively warm. A glacial age is not continuously cold but has many periods of varying temperatures and of varying degrees. We are about a fifth of the way into the current glacial age. During this period there have been about 20 periods of intense cold (glaciation) lasting 60 to 70 thousand years. The periods have been reasonably cyclic. Within each glaciation there are short periods of minor variation from the overall trend.

There are many contributing causes to ice ages with different influences. The major one is the shifting of the tectonic plates. The interior of the earth is (or at least contains) a molten layer of rock called the magma, which is kept hot by the intense pressure from gravity and heat from the radioactive decay of some elements, and when it reaches the surface, a volcano is formed. Cooling happens when little of the interior heat reaches the surface.

The amount of solar radiation striking the earth is also very important. The 24-degree tilt of the axis of rotation of the earth with respect to the plane of the orbit means that different parts of the surface receive different amounts of radiation during the orbit. The radiation received from the sun is not limited to the visible that we see, the infrared that we feel as heat, and the ultraviolet that causes sunburn and cancer. There is a wide range of radiation from the electromagnetic to a flux of mostly ionized particles known as the solar wind. This radiation would be lethal to life if all of it reached the surface. We are protected by two mechanisms. The first is the magnetic field of the earth that traps the ionized particles and deflects them to the magnetic poles, which is the source of the aurora borealis. The second mechanism is the atmosphere that blocks out some radiation. These two conditions are just a small part of the factors that have to be just right for life to exist. Mars, for example, has very little atmosphere not only because the weaker gravity cannot hold it but also because it has no magnetic field, and the solar wind blows away any that would form. In addition, the radiation of the sun varies due to processes taking place in it. We see this action as solar spots and solar storms.

In the current configuration, the North Pole, even though in the sea, is isolated from the oceans while the South Pole is a continent. Most of the land mass of the earth is in the northern hemisphere. Glaciation occurs mainly over land. This means the northern hemisphere has seen more effects than the southern hemisphere. The last ice age occurred about 20,000 years ago and was most intense in North America. The extent was as far south as the northern tier of states with an ice depth measured in kilometers. Some effects, of course, extended farther south. Most of the ice had melted by about 6,000 years ago. Many species of animals and plants became extinct. The great lakes and others were carved out. It is also why Minnesota has 10,000 lakes. Some species such as mastodons and wooly mammoths got caught in the ice and some frozen specimens were preserved though the species went extinct.

Ice ages have a large effect on everything. There were areas of high enough elevation to have remained above the ice; they would have provided islands of refuge for such organisms that were there or made it there. Other organisms would be wiped out. Certain flora could survive by seeds and pollen and able to stand the freeze. The last age was recent enough that it could have overlapped some biblical events. The Garden of Eden would not have survived so there is no use trying to locate it today. Some remnants of the last ice age are still with us. The Greenland ice cap and the Columbia ice field in western Canada are the most notable. Glaciers in the western North American mountains are examples and the glaciers of New Zealand. The melting of these features is partly due to coming out of that ice age. Living things produce heat and gases that can cause melting to accelerate. The human contribution is much discussed today. Although it is important, eliminating it would not stop melting because the other factors combine to continue the warming and melting process. In addition to trying to reduce the human component, provision should be made to adjust to it because the other factors will continue. We cannot change the solar effect; something on the sun could happen to cause drastic changes (this might have been a factor in some of the mass extinctions).

Volcanism is another issue not connected with Genesis or creation. At times in the earth's history there have been periods of intense volcanism. Evidence of this can be seen in many places as solidified lava beds, igneous rock formations, and ash deposits. The effect could be profound on life because the atmosphere could have been non-breathable or even toxic. The climate could have been hot from all of heat emitted or extremely cold from blocking out the sun's rays. We, have the present-day "ring of fire" of volcanoes in the Pacific region and other volcanoes worldwide and even a volcano in Antarctica. Many mountain ranges are of volcanic origin. There is no mention of volcanoes in the Bible, probably because there are few in the region. In New Testament times, the volcanoes of Italy must have been known as Mount Vesuvius did not bury Pompeii until 79 AD, but probably showed some activity before then. It is far away (for the times) from Egypt and Sinai.

The continental drift and tectonic plates are not explicitly described in the creation account. The concept was not even accepted until the second half of the twentieth century. The theory does explain some geographical features such as mountain building and earthquakes. Earthquakes are mentioned in the Bible and were present at Mt. Sinai while Moses was on the mountain. The action on Day 3 of the land separating from sea could have involved a similar process. Any equating of the two would be sheer speculation. What the theory does show is that land masses can move and different configurations of the earth's surface are not only possible, but have occurred in the past. It is just the description for the benefit of the Israelites at Sinai had to be in terms that they could understand. This means, among other things, that a time scale is not indicated and would have been of no interest.

In studying subatomic particles and their behavior, Werner Heisenberg discovered the startling fact now known as the uncertainty principle. It was first associated with the study of electrons but gradually become apparent in other circumstances. The idea originated in the early 1800s in the mathematical analysis of waves (in water, for example). The crest of the wave can, and usually does, move at a different velocity (faster) than the medium. The medium may not move at all, as described in an earlier chapter in the case of a "stadium" wave. Even various parts (positions) on the wave move at different velocities resulting in a spreading of the wave shape. The elementary wave form is known as a sine wave. It is obtained by plotting the value of the sine function from trigonometry. It is also the form one would get by plotting a point on the circumference of a circle if it were rolled along without slipping. Jean Baptiste Joseph Fourier, a French mathematician, developed the theory that any arbitrary wave form could be represented as a series of sine and cosine waves whose frequency (wavelength, wave number) are multiples of the composite wave frequency. The frequency of the wave that is the same as the original's is called the fundamental; the others all called harmonics. This technique has numerous applications in electrical engineering, sound analysis, and music theory. When the wave nature of a particle is being examined, its position is no longer precise because there is a probability of the particle being at any point on the wave. This is all mathematics, and extending to quantum physics, the product of the incremental position and the momentum is a constant. This means that in knowing one more precisely, the other is known less precisely. This is the crux of the Uncertainty principle. Scientists hate to admit there is something they cannot know.

There are other types of uncertainty in science (and lots of other fields). There is the uncertainty that comes from rounding off of numbers; that is, limiting the number of decimal points in a number. This is well understood and accepted. Do you really want to know that you weigh 176.374952 pounds, or is 176 good enough? Your scale may not display that many digits. The scale itself may not be that accurate; it has tolerance so that the actual weight might be anywhere between 174 and 178 if its accuracy is 1%. It could be even more. Also it may not read zero when there is no weight on it, which produces a bias. Important measuring instruments have some method of calibration to insure their accuracy. Precision is defined as to how many digits can be indicated, while accuracy is how correct those digits are and tolerance is the amount of uncertainty allowed.

Another source of uncertainty is that the very act of observing changes the conditions. Light is energy and shining it on an object exerts a force on the object. In everyday activities, the effect is too small to be of consequence but is very important in the subatomic realm and microbiology. A naturalist, in studying the behavior of creatures, may change their behavior by his presence. Extreme precautions must be used to minimize the disturbance. In measuring the temperature of a room precisely, your emitted body heat or the heat given off by the measuring device will change the temperature.

Archeologist and paleontologist have to be careful not to disturb sites being investigated or introduce contaminants. Some cannot be avoided, and the very act of excavation exposes the site to the atmosphere and all that is in it as well as increasing the oxidation.

Astronomical observations from satellites are more accurate and precise due to eliminating the effects from the atmosphere. There may be other effects in the space around the satellite as well.

To sum up, scientists are not nearly as certain of many things as they would like to be, think they are, or want you to believe they are. Still their studies, investigations, and experiments provide us with much useful knowledge of the universe in which we live.

15

Summary

A BRIEF SUMMARY CONCERNING GENESIS 1–3 and science: Genesis 1:1 says God created the heavens and the earth and science says the universe began with a big bang 10 to 14 billion years ago. (Both point to an origin from an unknown.) Genesis 1:2 says that the earth was without form and void, and science says that the earth formed 4.5 billion years ago in a state very inhospitable to life. Reluctantly, science says that the constants of the universe seem to be tailored to allow the development of life as we know it. This is known as the anthropic principle; atheists hate it. Genesis 1 hints at this. Genesis 1 also says that natural phenomena are the result of natural laws ordained by God and not under the capacious whims of gods. This makes it possible for humans to use their God-given intellect to study and understand those laws. From then on science and the Bible deal with two entirely different realms. The methods of study of each do not work in the study of the other. Science is an ever-changing landscape, so there is no reason to try to tie religion and science together. Where does a sense of morality come from? (Some atheists are trying to claim it is in the genetic code).

We need to ask ourselves the basic questions, such as "On what is my faith based?"; "Do I need absolute proof?"; "What would it take to destroy my faith?"; "Who am I?"; "Who do I want to be?"; "What do

I want?"; "Where am I going?"; and "Why am I here?" Science can't answer these questions, but the Bible can.

With scientists (and engineers) there is a certain way of thinking about things. Foremost is the belief that scientist's and engineer's brains are capable of solving problems. Some think that, given enough time and by doing enough investigation, they can come up with the correct answer to anything. Some even become very egotistical and arrogant. Most scientists do not like someone from another discipline encroaching on theirs. However, we do it all of the time. Evolutionists think the success they see for natural selection in biology can be extended to other disciplines. This includes things like sociology, psychology, economics, politics, or government. At times there is tension between micro or molecular biology and quantum physics. Both work at the smallest scale of matter.

Over the last 100 years, quantum physics has developed to deal with matter on the subatomic level where standard Newtonian mechanics break down. Quantum means that properties are not continuous but can only change in steps and even means that there is a lower limit, which is a heavily mathematical concept. One result has been the discovery that, in the very act of observing (a particle for example), the properties of the object being observed are changed. In observing an electron, knowing the momentum or position to a higher precision lowers the precision to which the other quality can be known. Mathematically, the product of the momentum and position is a constant for which a formula exists. The same is true for time and energy. This is known as the Heisenberg uncertainty principle, named after Werner Heisenberg who proposed it in 1927. It places an ultimate limit on our knowledge. Biologists don't like to apply this.

What I had hoped to show in this book was that science and religion are two separate areas with two different methodologies. Therefore, one cannot make claims about the other. For instance, that the Bible was written to certain people at certain times and had to be understandable by them, or that atheists have no grounds for denying the validity of religion and that religion (Christianity in particular) cannot invalidate science. In that context, Genesis is absolutely true and is very important in our spiritual development. The so-called conflicts are a smoke screen that diverts us from the real message.

In times past, people would ascribe any gap in scientific knowledge to a direct act of God. As more discoveries were made, this resulted in a smaller role for God. It ignores the difference between the material and the spiritual. Our faith should be based upon what we know, not upon what we don't know. The book of Genesis is telling us about the who of creation, not the details of how.

Our study of the Scriptures should overwhelm us with the love, concern, care, and provision that God has for us as His image. The awe and wonder should make us feel humble to even be considered by Him as passages, especially the Psalms, express. Our study of the physical universe should likewise create great awe and wonder (Rom. 1:19–21). We see how important, intricate details work together and the precision required for it to function at all. Learning about all of the things God has left for us to investigate should increase our faith rather than detract from it. The petty disputes over how the universe came about shrink into insignificance because they reveal our obsession with self and an overblown feeling of our own importance. I like the title Francis Collins gave to his book on the human genome: The Language of God. In a sense scientific discoveries are really just entries into the lexicon of the language of God. In the end, I like to think of the cosmic perspective given by Muller (see reference 9, page 338). After reviewing everything that we have been discussing in this book, there are only three legitimate prayers that we can have: Wow!, Thank You!, and Help!

References

1. A Brief History of Time, by Stephen W. Hawking. Bantam Books: New York, NY, 1988.
2. After the Ice Age, by E. C. Pielou. Univ. of Chicago Press: Chicago, IL, 1991.
3. Bible: various versions: RSV, NRSV, NIV, The Message, ASV.
4. Can a Darwinian Be a Christian?, by Michael Ruse. Cambridge Univ. Press: Cambridge, UK, 2001.
5. Finding Darwin's God, by Kenneth R. Miller. HarperCollins Books: New York, NY, 1999.
6. Five Equations that Changed the World, by Michael Guillen. Hyperion: New York, NY, 1995.
7. History of the Hour, by Gerhard Dohrn-Van Rossum (translated by Thomas Dunlap). Univ. of Chicago Press, 1996
8. Hyperspace, by Michio Kaku. Anchor Books: New York, NY, 1994.
9. Now: The Physics of Time, by Richard Muller. W. W. Norton & Company: New York, NY, 2016.
10. Telecosm, by George Gilder. Free Press: New York, NY, 2000.
11. The Constants of Nature, by John D. Barrow. Pantheon Books: New York, NY, 2002.
12. The Discovery of Time, edited by Stuart McCready. SourceBooks: Naperville, IL, 2001.

13. The Language of God, by Francis S. Collins. Free Press: New York, NY, 2006.

14. The Lost World of Adam and Eve, by John H. Walton. InterVarsity Press: Downers, Grove, IL, 2015.

15. The Lost World of Genesis One, by John H. Walton. InterVarsity Press: Downers Grove, IL, 2009.

16. Time Lord, by Clark Blaise. Vintage Books: New York, NY, 2000.

17. Young's Analytical Concordance to the Bible, 22nd ed. by Robert Young. Eerdmans: Grand Rapids, Michigan, 1964, 1969, 1970, reprinted 1975.

18. The website http://nobelists.net has a free e-book, 50 Nobel Laureates Who Believe in God.

19. Numerous websites for the following topics: Egyptian mythology, geological ages, mass extinctions, Big Bang theory, theory of relativity (special and general), radioactivity—elements, half-lives, periodic table of the elements, uncertainty principle, anthropic principle, gravity, quantum theory, quantum entanglement, particles of physics, and genome. University websites are usually the best. Be cautious of Wikipedia because it can be user edited. Be aware that cosmology, particle (quantum) physics, and genetics are being edited rapidly.

20. The American Scientific Affiliation: http://network.asa3.org. "We in the American Scientific Affiliation believe that God is both the creator of our vast universe and the source of our ability to pursue knowledge—also, that honest and open studies of both Scripture and nature are mutually beneficial in developing a full understanding of human identity and our environment. ASA members are both scientists and Christians."

21. Searching for the Oldest Stars by Anna Frebel. Princeton University Press: Princeton, NJ, 2015.

Appendix

SEVERAL TOPICS ARE GIVEN HERE that most people will be familiar with. They are discussed here so that they will not clutter up the main text and so that those who are not familiar with them need not be lost or confused.

A note on notation and symbols: Sciences, mathematics, engineering, and other fields use a lot of symbols and acronyms to make expressions and manipulation of formulas and operations less wieldy, but it results in making it more difficult to understand by someone outside the field. The alphabet is a popular source of symbols; there are 26 upper case letters and 26 lower case letters. This does not make for 52 symbols because the upper and lower cases of a few letters are hard to distinguish although they all may still be used. To increase the count of symbols, the Greek alphabet, upper and lower case, is extensively used, although some are the same as Roman characters and some are not easily written, so less than 48 separate symbols are available. There are also some symbols that are created. The same symbol may have different meanings in different fields (or even in the same field). Where possible, a character is chosen to relate to what is being represented, using the first letter of the term. From high school algebra we are all familiar with using x, y, and z as variables and labels for the axes of a graph. An important part of learning a new field is learning the definition of terms and the appropriate symbols.

Scientific and engineering terms have precise definitions that are not always distinguished in common usage. Some terms have only a magnitude associated with them (a scalar number) while others include a direction (a vector). Speed is a scalar and velocity is a vector, but many people use them interchangeably. Acceleration is a vector and may indicate a changing direction but not speed. Mass and weight are not identical because weight includes units of acceleration due to gravity, with $W=mg$, where W is the weight, m is the mass, and g is the acceleration due to gravity. Common usage almost always uses weight where mass in meant.

A note on scientific notation for numbers: Those who work with extremely small or extremely large numbers use a shorthand rather than having to write out many zeros. This is done by using powers of 10. Ten itself is just 10 to the first power, 100 is 10 to the second power, 1,000 is 10 to the third power, etc., and are written as 10^1, 10^2, 10^3, and following. A number is written as a figure less than 10 followed by a decimal point and whatever digits are required for the precision wanted multiplied by a power of 10. For example; 186,000 is written as 1.86×10^5; the 1.86 are called the significant digits. For numbers less than one, the significant digits are multiplied by 10 with a negative exponent meaning divide by that power of 10. This saves having to write zeros after the decimal point, thus 0.000000321 becomes 3.21×10^{-7}. To multiply two numbers simply multiply the significant digits and add the exponents of 10, paying attention to the sign of the exponent. Thus 186,000 times 0.000000321 becomes $1.86 \times 3.21 \times 10^{5-7} = 5.9706 \times 10^{-2}$ $= 0.059706$. (Engineers will usually round off the significant digits to those that are really needed like making 5.9706 just 5.97 depending on how precise the original numbers were. In the "dark ages" when slide rules were used for calculations; they were only good to three significant digits and the user had to keep track of the decimal point. Also the user learned to make a quick estimate of the result to catch errors. (This skill is still useful with calculators or computers.). To divide numbers the significant digits are divided, the sign of the exponent of the divisor is changed, and the exponents added. Thus 1.86×10^5 divided by 3.21 $\times 10^{-7}$ becomes $1.86/3.21 \times 10^{5-(-7)}$, or $0.57943 \ldots \times 10^{12}$, or 5.79×10^{11}.

When dealing with imprecise numbers it is useful to use the term "on the order of . . .," which is usually a factor of 10. Thus "on the order of 100" could mean anything between 50 and 500. To say the "magnitude of X" usually means closer to X but some people use these terms interchangeably.

A note on atomic theory: The theory that all matter is made up of very small particles, surprisingly, has had a rather recent general acceptance. An ancient Greek philosopher actually proposed a theory (using solid spheres as the model) about the time of Christ but it didn't get much press. The model we are familiar with was proposed by Niels Bohr in the early 1900s, for which he won the Nobel Prize in physics. It consists of three subatomic particles: a positively charged proton, a negatively charged electron, and a neutrally charged neutron. The weight of the neutron is slightly heavier than the proton that is about 1,860 times the weight of the electron and the atom is similar to a planetary system. The core or nucleus contains protons and neutrons with the electrons orbiting like planets around a sun. Normally each type of element has the same number of protons and electrons and is thus electrically neutral. For all elements except hydrogen, the nucleus contains neutrons. The atomic number of an element is the number of protons in the nucleus. The atomic weight is the number of protons plus the number of neutrons. If an element has members with different numbers of neutrons, they are called isotopes. Like magnets, atomic particles of the same polarity repel, and those of opposite polarity attract. The protons should repel each other but there is another force called the strong nuclear force that holds them together, along with the neutrons. In some isotopes the force is not quite sufficient so the nucleus is unstable. Different isotopes disintegrate in different ways by giving off particles or energy (actually called "decay") and at different rates. The process changes one isotope into another, or more often into a different element. To measure this rate of change, the time required for half of the mass of a given sample to change is the "half-life." The decay of a given atom cannot be predicted, only a statistical distribution of the times. It is possible to trigger the decay of an atom by adding extra protons and/or neutrons to the nucleus.

Quantum theory states that the orbits of the electrons around a nucleus are restricted to certain (quantum) levels. For an electron to jump from one level to another (or be expelled entirely), energy must be absorbed or emitted. If an electron (or more) is ejected, the atom is left with a net positive change, and if an extra one (or more) is added, the atom has a net positive charge. Charged atoms are known as ions.

Light or other radiation is emitted or energy absorbed during quantum transitions.

Further research has concluded that protons and neutrons are made up of smaller particles called quarks. A veritable zoo of fundamental particles has now been postulated. Most of the subatomic particles are too small to possibly be seen by current imaging devices that are wavelength limited. Some are proposed to fit the mathematical formulas of theories. (An example is the graviton to explain gravity.) Experimental verification has to be detected using the effects rather than the actual particle. The question then becomes, "What is the makeup of this batch of particles?" The latest step is that they are not physical matter but waves of energy and that every physical body has a wave function that contains the information about it. The study of them requires very complicated (to most of us) mathematics.

A note on units of measure: When we want to describe something, we employ a measurement of some property of it. Through the ages, myriads of systems of measurement have been used, often unique to a particular area. The confusion can be considerable as different groups of people with different systems interact with one another. Even for the same unit of measurement, differences occur depending on the standard used. Because of the influence as the British Empire spread, English units were widely used (there is still the problem of a standard). The French took the lead in the 1800s to use a worldwide system. This evolved into today's metric system which is used for almost all scientific measurements. The basic unit of length in the meter, originally defined as one ten millionth of the distance from the equator to the North Pole. You see that where and how you actually measure is subject to variations. The British and the Americans came up with slightly different values but the world's standard is still a bar of metal kept in a controlled environment in Paris. The laboratory standard is a given number of wave-lengths of light emitted by atoms of a certain element.

A degree of temperature used in the sciences is defined using pure water at the air pressure present at sea level. The point where water freezes is 0 and where water boils is 100. The scale is divided into 100 equal degrees. The original name was "centigrade" for obvious reasons but later changed to "Celsius" to honor the person who first promoted it. The Fahrenheit scale was based on less precise phenomena but we still use it in the United States for common purposes. (Lots of units in science are named after people even though the original would be easier to image, as in changing "cycles per second" to "Hertz.") For some calculations, the temperature is referenced to absolute zero. This is the temperature at which all molecular motion stops (-273.15 °C or -459.67 °F). The scale with 0° at absolute zero and the size of a degree the same as for Celsius is called °Kelvin. The gram is the weight of one cubic centimeter of pure water at 4 degrees C. The second originally came as a division of a minute (or hour, day, year, whatever). Now it is based on the frequency of emitted radiation from a certain atom. With addition of the charge on an electron, all other units are derived from these fundamental ones. The metric system is often referred to as the cgs (centimeter-gram-second) or MKS (meter-kilogram-second) system. Mass and weight do not have the same units because weight involves units of acceleration from Newton's law, F=ma.

All measurement systems had in common that they were anthropocentric, that is, they were convenient for the size of humans. As other units were derived, some of them became unwieldy for everyday things. Thus were added various prefixes that we use today, such as kilo, mega, giga, micro, or nano. For the very large (cosmology) and the very small (quantum physics), more convenient units were named: angstrom (10^{-8} centimeters) for atoms and light years (the distance light travels in a vacuum in one year; 186,000 miles per second, times 3,600 seconds per hour, times 24 hours per day, times 365.4 days per year—try that on your handheld calculator—5.88×10^{12} miles) for cosmology (a parsec is 3.26 lightyear). This all can be very tricky, so one has to be careful.

A note about entropy: Entropy is a term originally coined to measure the efficiency of steam engines. It is mysterious in that we cannot see it, feel it, or sense it in normal ways. In fact, it is a virtual concept derived mathematically to handle problems in design of engines. The Britannica Online Encyclopedia says entropy "provides deep insight into the direction of spontaneous change for many everyday phenomena." In some sense it is a measure of the energy that is unavailable to do work. The units are a system's thermal energy per unit temperature. Because temperature is a measure of molecular motion (and hence, kinetic energy) and work is obtained from ordered molecular motion, entropy is viewed as a measure of molecular disorder. The concept has been applied as a measure of disorder or randomness in many everyday systems. It can show the impossibility of processes that appear to violate no other physical law.

At the initial onset of creation, whether you view it from the Big Bang or as an act of God, everything was compact and ordered so that the entropy was zero or very small because everything was well ordered. As the universe expanded, the disorder increased. The defining equation, because the concept arose in the design of steam engines, has to do with the flow of heat. Heat will always naturally flow from a body (solid, gaseous, or otherwise) of higher temperature, T_H, to one of lower temperature, T_L. Heat, in thermodynamics, is indicated by Q and entropy by S. The temperatures are given in degrees Kelvin (absolute zero being zero degrees). The formula for the change in entropy is $S=Q(1/T_H-1/T_L)$.

Some examples help explain the idea. In a steam engine, water is boiled to produce steam that expands. If it is confined, then the pressure in the containment vessel increases. The steam is vented into a cylinder containing a (moveable) piston. As the piston moves, the steam expands, cools and condenses to water (the work is done by the piston). The water is then returned and again boiled. Energy must be expended to boil the water; from burning fuel or heat from a nuclear reaction, and the cycle begins again. Internal combustion engines work the same way, except high pressure gases are produced by exploding the fuel. Refrigeration works by removing heat. In this case the heat causes a gas at pressure to expand, which lowers the temperature of the gas. The heat must be dumped somewhere, for an air conditioner it dumps heat into the atmosphere. The temperature of the room is cooled, but that of the universe is increased. Likewise, the entropy of the room is decreased, but the entropy of the universe is increased by a larger amount. (Work had to be done to compress the gas.)

The concept became useful in describing other situations in which something ordered is disordered in which entropy is increased or vice versa, in which entropy in decreased. To order something requires work that increases entropy of the complete system. Having a container of cold water and a container of hot water is an ordered system with low entropy. Mix the two together and you have a disordered system; the entropy is higher because you cannot separate the hot and cold. It would take work to again have water with the separate conditions. In general, producing an ordered system (such as manufacturing something) reduces the entropy of the system but at the expense of increasing entropy of the environment. Jesus describes entropy being created in Matthew 6:19 when He says that "moth and rust destroy" your treasures on earth.

As the universe expands and becomes more uniform the entropy increases. That is why the second law of thermodynamics states that the entropy, the disorder of the universe, is increasing and will continue to increase forever. If things continue as they are now, the universe will eventually reach a uniform cold temperature. Long before that happens however the sun will use all of its nuclear fuel, collapse into a super nova, explode, and envelope all of the solar system. Or Christ will return before then.

The first chapter of Genesis describes how God is ordering our particular region of the universe to produce the solar system and forming the earth to make in suitable for human habitation. If scientists discover the details of the process, so be it.

Order Information

RELIANT
PUBLISHING
A DIVISION OF REDEMPTION PRESS

To order additional copies of this book, please visit
www.redemption-press.com.
Also available on Amazon.com, BarnesandNoble.com,
Or by calling toll free 1-844-2REDEEM.

CPSIA information can be obtained
at www.ICGtesting.com
Printed in the USA
LVHW030607100221
678886LV00006B/576